# THE **LONGEST** CAMPAIGN

*Facing the Challenge – Learning the Lessons
of Life Threatening West Nile Virus*

*By*
KEN SUMMERS

## Endorsements

"A gritty, authentic page turner, this book is guaranteed to inspire both faith and faithfulness, and remind us again that God will be with us when we walk through the shadow lands."

Jeff Lucas,

Author, Speaker, Broadcaster

"Ken Summers writes with the authenticity of a person who has won significant victories, overcome setbacks and walked through the 'valley of the shadow of death.' This is the inspiring story of a great man of God, sustained by faith and his family, who has survived grievous hardships with optimism, intellectual vitality and spiritual power."

Bill Armstrong, President

Colorado Christian University

Former US Senator

"I am honored to endorse Ken's book. As one of his medical doctors I witnessed firsthand how many times Ken faced death right in the eye and found a way to conquer it. The only way to explain it all is that his soul was fed by his faith and the Holy Spirit."

Dr. Daniel Asadi

Medical Director

Northern Colorado Long Term Acute Hospital

"Some books inspire. Some are windows to the soul. Some are practical. Some are so visceral about thoughts and feelings in times of great trial that the reader is captured. Ken Summers' *The Longest Campaign* is all of that and more. If you want to know God better, read this book. If you want encouragement in time of great distress and uncertainty, read this book. If you want to know what faithfulness and devotion in marriage looks like, read this book. Ken and Debbie Summers' story lifts our sights to another place!"

Dick Foth<br>
Pastor/Author<br>
Minister-at-Large to the Congressional Community<br>
Washington, D.C.

"I've long admired Ken's ability to take a simple story and turn it into a compelling tale. Yet there is nothing simple about the story of his fight against a fluke encounter with life-threatening illness. Ken's faith has consistently been a source of strength for all of us who know and love him. Even as his faith was tested through mental and physical trials, he remained committed to his family, our faith and his recovery. He is a remarkable man and his story is an inspiration. A wonderful read that allows a pleasantly candid view into the roller-coaster life of a great man."

Rep. Frank McNulty<br>
Speaker of the Colorado House of Representative (2011-2012)

"Ken Summers gives us an inspiring self-portrait of an un-compartmentalized life, a man in full. Too many of us keep our commitments to faith, family, and freedom in separate boxes. Not Ken. Whether in ministry, politics, or battling a mysterious illness, his lifework has been all of one piece — fearlessly testifying to the reasons for his hope in Christ, standing with the great cloud of witnesses. Summers' book goes on my shelf alongside Shackleton's story in *Endurance* and Zamperini's in *Unbroken* — each a landmark of victory through indomitable courage."

Senator John Andrews<br>
Former President, Colorado Senate<br>
Founder, Western Conservative Summit<br>
Author/Political Think Tank Founder

"Paul tells the Corinthian church that the 'quality of everyone's work will be tested and revealed by fire.' Ken Summers has been put through a fiery ordeal by his harrowing encounter with the West Nile disease. *The Longest Campaign* reveals how the Lord empowered Ken and his wife Debbie to emerge from that ordeal on a foundation of gold. It is a story that will challenge and encourage your faith. I urge you to read it and be better prepared for your test, whatever it may be."

Rep. Spencer Swalm
Colorado State Representative (2007-2014)

"Ken Summers has shared with us a story of challenges, setbacks, and personal reinvention that is held together by the constancy of his character. Pulled forward by faith, family, the generosity of his service, and gratitude for those that served him, Ken gives us a guide to finding the affirmative in the most difficult struggles. Having served with Ken in the Colorado House of Representatives, I always believed that his work there fully proved his mettle. Ken shows it was merely preparation for the real physical and spiritual struggles that can face us all. His courage and commitment show through in this book, and it is well worth seeking its inspiration."

Senator Andy Kerr
Colorado State Senator

"Wow! Talk about a journey of faith. I have personally watched Ken and Debbie walk through this challenging season. I have seen unwavering faith, absolute determination, complete dependence on God and firm resolve. This book will strengthen you and encourage you in times of doubt, fear or suffering. A must read!"

Dary Northrop, Lead Pastor
Timberline Church
Fort Collins, CO

"An excellent, well-written story of life taking a sharp turn we weren't anticipating! Ken Summers tells this riveting story in a fresh, candid way that pulls us into the story. His serious physical challenges that began in the summer of 2013, compounded by other complications and infections, drove him and his incredible wife, Debbie, to depend upon their family, their friends, and their faith in God in ways never imagined. This book will encourage those going through deep valleys of physical or emotional suffering."

Bob Cook, Lead Pastor
Victory Life Church
Grand Junction, CO

"It has been said character is defined not by your *actions,* but by your <u>re</u>-*actions*; your reactions not only to success but to adversity as well. I first met Ken Summers the summer of 1980 when he was a youth pastor in Lakewood, Colorado. I watched with admiration the abundance of integrity and character Ken displayed through success reached as he grew in ministry, higher education and then in politics. Even more so the depth of character he is displaying after encountering incredible physical hardships. As you read these pages, may this book enlighten, challenge and encourage you."

Tim Brotzman
Radio Host/Author
Former radio host 560 KLZ
KOSI 101.1 FM
National Show-Jones Radio Network

"Ken Summers' story of his medical journey through contracting the life-threatening West Nile Virus is an exhilarating walk of faith. When one realizes that Ken is alive today through the loving and prayerful support of family and friends it is nothing but amazing and truly exemplifies the resurrection power of God. Ken has been a long-time friend and colleague through the Teen Challenge ministry and as a former state legislator in Colorado. Ken was highly respected across the nation in Teen Challenge. As you read Ken's book, *The Longest Campaign*, I'm sure, like me, you'll be moved by Ken's trust in God that encapsulates the true meaning of faith that each of us can draw strength from."

Rev. Snow Peabody
Executive State Director, Teen Challenge of Arizona
National Representative to Washington, D.C.
Teen Challenge USA

# Dedication

This book is dedicated to my wife Debbie. She has stood by my side for forty years and by my bedside when I needed her most. It is no exaggeration to say that her diligence literally saved my life, on more than one occasion. Also to my children, Christian and Stephanie, who, with their spouses and children, provided the support and made the sacrifices that demonstrated loyalty and love.

# CONTENTS

# Acknowledgments

I am grateful for the many who encouraged me to take on this effort and those who provided the support my family and I needed to survive my health crisis. This book is as much their story as it is mine.

In addition to my wife and children and their families, my mother, brother and sister and their families and my brother and sister-in-law, there were many from my extended family who visited, prayed, and encouraged me on and rejoiced in my progress.

I am thankful for the support of our friends Craig and Cyndy Luzinski. Craig and Cyndy had been neighbors to Debbie's mother and had become our friends as well. Both of them have nursing backgrounds. In the early days of my hospitalization, they were the first to suggest I had West Nile infection.

I was humbled by the support of almost 175 individuals who contributed to my "Medical Relief Fund." This has provided resources for ongoing medical services needed for a lengthy recovery, insurance deductibles and copayments. My friends from Teen Challenge, Gina Brummett and Janel Bryan, helped with the set up and oversight of this fund.

I am also grateful to the Board of Teen Challenge and Gina Brummett, Deputy Director, who stepped in to ensure the organization ran smoothly and took on the responsibility of some challenging decisions during my hospitalization.

The support from the Colorado General Assembly was most appreciated and overwhelming. Several of my legislative colleagues came to visit me in the hospital. Many of these were part of the Tuesday morning Bible study for legislators conducted by Chaplain Dan File. I have had the opportunity in the last two years to open a session of the House in prayer and have always been graciously received. The outpouring of support in so many ways is humbling. I am thankful to former House Speakers Frank McNulty and Mark Ferindino and current Speaker Dickey Lee Hullinghorst.

I am thankful for the prayers and support from many churches in Colorado and around the country, especially those Debbie and I had a personal connection with including Timberline Church, Fort Collins; Dakota Ridge Assembly, Littleton; Foothills Bible Church, Littleton; and the Day by Day Sunday School Class of Southern Gables Church, Littleton. I appreciated the opportunity to share my first message in many years at Southwest First Assembly in Lakewood where my friend Jim Brummett is the pastor. Red Rocks Fellowship and Pastor Jack McCullough also provided me an opportunity to share my thanks for their support and a testimony of my experience.

In addition to churches that I knew were praying for me, I was humbled to learn of the consistent support in prayer from Senator Bill Armstrong, President of Colorado Christian University, and his leadership team. On several occasions, he made reference to how I was prayed for by his team, as he met with his leaders and provided an update on my condition.

I am also thankful for the support of my friends and teammates from the Lakewood Cougars Senior Softball Team. I was hospitalized right at the end of our regular season and missed the last few games and the tournament. Our team won our league title. It was a special time when some of the team members came to my home and presented me with my T-Shirt recognizing our league championship.

In Chapter 8 of this book, I share some of the "divine" and unexpected sources of help that came to my family and me during my illness. There were so many who came to visit, and who expressed their support that it is difficult to recognize and thank them all personally. Each visit and expression of concern is not taken for granted. These individuals took the time and drove the many miles needed to come to a hospital in northern Colorado. I realize that is no small commitment. Thank you from the bottom of my heart for your love and encouragement to be an overcomer.

I am thankful for all those who assisted in reviewing and editing my manuscript. I am especially grateful for the work of Drenda Thoen, my colleague with the Larimer Energy Action Project.

Finally, I am most humbled by the presence, strength and encouragement of my Lord and Savior who was faithful in revealing Himself in so many ways at just the right time. I join with the Apostle Paul in saying,

> *"Now to the King eternal, immortal, invisible, the only*
> *God, be honor and glory forever and ever. Amen." —*
> *1 Timothy 1:17 (NIV)*

# Introduction

While attending a church service, I heard the saying, "When you share your story, you own your story." Perhaps that got my attention because there is so much of my health crisis and days in intensive care that have been erased from my memory. It was months after I returned home from the hospital before I began to read some of the Caring Bridge entries that chronicled my "forgotten days." In many ways it was hard for me to comprehend what I read truly happened to me.

During my initial hospitalization, I faced many days when my outcome was uncertain. I experienced total paralysis, brain trauma, respiratory failure, weeks on life support and a major surgery. In the process, I lost forty pounds, and most of my muscle mass. I went from 172 pounds, with a body mass index of about fourteen percent, to 132 pounds. I remember lying in bed and looking at my legs and realized my knees were bigger than my thighs. It had been almost two months before I realized I had not looked in a mirror during that entire time. I recall wheeling myself into the bathroom and looking at myself in the mirror. I hardly recognized the emaciated face and body that I observed.

Through the nearly five months of hospitalization, therapists of all kinds worked with me to restore lung function, the ability to swallow, cognitive ability and rebuild muscles and mobility. This included respiratory therapists, physical therapists, occupational therapists, speech therapists and wound care specialists. I would spend an unprecedented sixty days in inpatient rehabilitation until returning home to continue my recovery.

As I emerged from my health crisis, many people, besides my mother, encouraged me to write a book. I wasn't sure if that was anything I would take on, but I have come to realize sharing your story not only helps you own our story, but it can serve as a source of encouragement to others; that is certainly my goal and purpose in taking on this task.

In the pages that follow, I share much of the story of my professional life as a pastor, state representative and executive director of Teen Challenge of the Rocky Mountains. What I have found is the experiences of life prepare you for what you experience in life. You don't encounter a crisis and automatically learn to trust God to see you through. You are more equipped to face those times if you have a history of confidence in the Lord's direction and provision that serves as a foundation for your life. You don't have the supportive relationships that are needed to help and encourage you in a time of crisis if you have not invested in people and valued relationships.

I also communicate some of the "lessons learned" from my experience; to experience a health crisis and not be changed is a waste of suffering. I have come to realize "you don't know what you can go through until you have to go through it." Many people ask me how I made it through my months of hospitalization and lengthy recovery. I believe it was a manifestation of God's grace and strength, the support of my wife and family and the answer to many prayers. My daughter tells me, with a laugh, "When you didn't do well, we just gave you meds." I'm not sure if I have a comprehensive grasp on all that I have learned through my experience, but there are certainly some "high points" I believe are important to share and for others to consider.

Finally, at the end of the book, you will find a section of devotionals I have written on my road to recovery. An unexpected outcome of my illness has been updates or blog devotionals that have been written every day for over two years. These can be found on my website at www.kensummers.org

These should be read as daily devotionals. I trust that in doing so, what I share from my perspective of scriptural insight through the lens of my experience will challenge and strengthen your faith and trust in the Lord. Some devotionals are found in the main text at the end of a relevant chapter.

At this time, I am still in my recovery process. I have not regained full mobility and still lack strength and range of motion in my arms and shoulders. However, I find I am still committed to waging the campaign of trust in the Lord and perseverance toward my ultimate goal of full recovery. My prayer is that in your life, you will discover what I have: "What the Lord doesn't keep us from, He is able to see us through."

*Chapter 1*

# The Last Campaign

I t was election night 2012. My family and I gathered with friends and supporters at a local golf course clubhouse. We anxiously waited for the initial results of the election. I had served six years in the Colorado House and now I was in a campaign for a highly contested seat in the Colorado Senate in a newly drawn Senate District.

The campaign pitted me against another House colleague in the only political race in the state that had two House members competing for the same seat. It was a long and arduous campaign. The attack ads against me were vicious and relentless. They not only distorted my record and views, but also some of my fundamental personal beliefs and values.

I had felt honored to serve the citizens of Colorado's House District 22, which was located in south Lakewood and a portion of south Jefferson County. I served six years on the House Education Committee and in my last term I served as the Chair of the House Health and Environment Committee. Those two committees had legislative oversight of departments that comprised two-thirds of the state budget.

My journey to elective office was an interesting one. I had started my career as a high school business teacher and coach and then served almost twenty-eight years in local church ministry. I served congregations in Strasburg, Colorado, Colby, Kansas and Lakewood, Colorado.

As 2006 approached my wife Debbie and I felt a change coming to our pastoral ministry. I had just finished my Master of Nonprofit Management Degree from Regis University in Denver. In addition to my pastoral position, I had served on the Board of Teen Challenge of the Rocky Mountains and at the time worked on establishing a nonprofit to provide mentors to children of prisoners. At this time, many churches launched nonprofits under the encouragement from President George W. Bush's "Faith-Based and Community Initiatives" effort.

My plan for the future was to focus on my own nonprofit interests and serve as a consultant to other nonprofits and churches in their community outreach efforts. At the same time, an unexpected opportunity arose for me to run for the nomination of Sate Representative. I in the back of mind, I had an interest in serving in the State House and I received encouragement from some friends and some key political individuals in my area.

Since we planned a transition, Debbie and I felt that it would be worth approaching the opportunity to run for public office one step at a time. There were five individuals vying for the nomination to be the Republican candidate for the upcoming general election. My decision was fraught with some restless nights, much anxiety and a lot of work, but in the process, I felt energized by the experience. I felt it would be a good experience and opportunity for personal growth regardless of what took place.

By the time the local delegates made their decision, I was selected as the candidate for the general election. It was not anticipated to be a good year for Republicans nationally or in Colorado. My opponent was a popular young teacher who was well funded by various interest groups. I was committed to working hard and with some last minute help from some outside groups I won that election and began my public service as a State Representative. I was one of a few Republicans elected in highly competitive seat. The incoming class of freshman legislators for the 2007 legislative session was the largest group of new members since Colorado statehood.

As Election Day 2012 came, I faced the results of my fourth political campaign. There was a lot of uncertainty, but I had worked hard and anticipated a close race. Since many voters take advantage of mail ballots and early voting, the outcome of many elections is evident with the first report from the County Clerk's office. A friend of mine had indicated if I was within 800 votes of my opponent on the first report, then I would have a good chance of winning.

The mood in the clubhouse restaurant was upbeat and positive. My daughter and her husband had flown in from Atlanta to join us for the final days leading up to the election. My son monitored the computer and waited for the initial ballot "dump."

I was busy in conversation when Christian called me over to the corner where he manned the computer. "Dad, you need to take a look at this." It took a few moments for the numbers and the reality to set in. The initial report had me down by 2,000 votes! My heart sank, but I tried to ignore the inevitable for a few moments and hope there could be a change in the numbers.

It wasn't long before I realized I needed to address those who were gathered to thank them for their support during the campaign and to announce my opponent would be serving as their new State Senator and not me.

During the campaign, I tried to prepare myself for the fact that this could be my last campaign for public office. I felt that if that happened, I could feel good about having served for six years as one of 100 individuals who make up the State House and Senate and pass laws for the five million citizens of Colorado. It appeared my last campaign with all the hard work, opposition, relationships and character-testing challenges had come to an end. Now, it was time to face the reality that a change was in store for Debbie and me. We needed to prepare to chart a new future, just as we had done in the early years of our marriage when we made a move from teaching into full-time ministry.

## Chapter 2

# A Time for Change

Officially my term of office as a State Representative lasted until the swearing in of my successor. That took place in the early days of 2013. The New Year brought an end to one phase of life and the beginning of another. Those times can be filled with a sense of anticipation, whether they happen by choice or by default. We had faced those times before.

Debbie and I met as students at the University of Northern Colorado in Greeley. She was from Fort Collins; I was from Englewood. We met at the local Assemblies of God church we both attended as incoming college freshmen.

We were married in Fort Collins on June 19, 1976 after I graduated with my degree in Business Education. Debbie still had a few more credits and internships to finish before she completed her requirements for a Bachelor of Science in nursing. We moved into a rented house owned by my uncle close to Denver's Washington Park and I began my teaching career at my old high school in Englewood. Even though we lived within walking distance of Full Gospel Chapel (now Orchard Road Christian Center), the church I had grown up in, we began attending First Assembly in Lakewood to establish "our" church as newlyweds.

Over the next two years as our involvement in our local church grew, I felt a "call" to full-time ministry. Debbie's parents had been briefly in pastoral ministry after they finished their studies at Central Bible Institute in Springfield, Missouri. While they did not continue in vocational ministry they ended up serving as members and leaders of their local Assemblies of God church (Timberline Church) in Fort Collins for over fifty years.

I was just offered my third teaching contract. That meant I would be a "tenured" teacher after completing my third year. When we shared with Debbie's parents about our plans to leave the security of our current position for full-time ministry, they were supportive but cautious. "If you can do anything else, do it!" was the comment from Debbie's mother. The comment wasn't so much to discourage, but to test the sincerity of our "call" and plans.

The church we attended had part-time pastors and interns in the past, but never a full-time youth pastor. Tom Goins, the Senior Pastor, was from Oklahoma and had been at the church for two years. He had a nephew with the same teaching background as mine, who had gone into ministry. Tom himself had gone into ministry from secular employment. He proved to be a great encouragement, displaying patience and seeing potential in me that I did not see in myself at the time.

The church grew and Tom felt the church would be in a position to hire a full-time youth pastor in the fall of 1978. So, with a sense of excitement in taking a "step of faith" and even though we expected our first child in the fall, I informed the administrators at my school that I would not accept a teaching contract for the coming school year.

As the current school year ended, I continued my work at the church along with my work at a small sign company that was owned by Morris Vogel, a teacher from Arapahoe High School in Littleton whom I had served with as a student teacher. Debbie worked in a doctor's office for a family physician. For a newlywed couple, life was manageable.

It was in July of 1978, when Tom Goins informed me that he had accepted a position as the new Senior Pastor of a large Assembly of God in Broken Arrow, Oklahoma. This was a strong church with a great history in Oklahoma and it certainly was a good opportunity. We quickly learned how the opportunity for one could place in jeopardy the plans of another. Unfortunately, we were the ones whose plans were suddenly unsure, more than ever.

It was during this time that Debbie and I found the sense of peace that can accompany you in the midst of the challenges of life. Even though the future had more questions than answers and there was a great deal of uncertainty, we had a subtle sense of peace that our lives were in God's hands and everything would be okay. At the time we didn't realize how the sense of spiritual calm and confidence, in the face of grave uncertainty, would once again be tested over three decades later.

During the following weeks we did what we thought would be prudent in exploring our "Plan B." The fall was approaching, my final salary from my teaching contract would come to an end in August and a final decision about our future had not been made, although it appeared the church board had narrowed the choice for a new senior pastor. It was during this time I received a call from a minister by the name of James Majeske from Michigan. He had served as the District Youth Director of the Assemblies of God in Michigan. His wife Carolyn was a Colorado native from Pueblo. He had plans to return to pastoral ministry and was interested in coming to Colorado. Since I served as a youth pastor, I was excited about the prospects, but it felt "too little, too late" to become a reality.

A recent edition of a national youth magazine had a picture of District Youth leaders from across the country. I took it to the chair of the Deacon Board, and pointed out James Majeske in the picture, identifying him as the one who called. The Board did delay its final decision and interviewed the Majeske's for the position. I still remember a lengthy phone conversation with James during his time of consideration. It appeared we shared the same values and philosophies when it came to ministry. I continued to perform "pastoral duties" during the interim, awaiting a final decision. During this time, the church even gained a few new families who remained with the church for a number of years.

When the end of September approached, James Majeske received the vote and call to become the new senior pastor. I realized someone in his position knew a multitude of good and experienced youth pastors who probably would be glad to come to Colorado. So my hopes for the future still felt dim.

During one final phone, James concluded by commenting about Debbie expecting a baby the next month and that considering the fact he was returning to local church ministry after serving in a district-wide position for seven years, he felt it would be wise to keep us on staff and to work out the full-time position and to "give it a try for a year." Pastor's Majeske's first Sunday at Lakewood First Assembly was the final Sunday of October in 1978, two days after the birth of our first child.

This chain of events, once again, taught us some invaluable lessons that would be needed in the future. We learned the importance of taking one day at a time, continuing to do what you can, while trusting the Lord to do what you can't and knowing the Lord always comes through. It has been observed, "The Lord is always on time, but He misses some great opportunities to be early."

I continued to serve on staff with James Majeske for four years. During this time our daughter was born in 1980. Also, my ministry role and responsibilities changed over those years and the lessons I learned would be of great value to me in my future ministry. At one time, the connection between the two of us felt like it could continue into a long-term ministry team.

One day in one of my many conversations with James, he told me, "Ken, I know we have discussed being together as a team for the long haul, but, I believe there are some gifts and abilities that you will never develop unless you become a pastor of your own church. I would like to present that to you as a challenge and a matter of prayer." I accepted his challenge with anxiety mixed with anticipation and began to make my future a matter of prayer and consideration. Sooner than anticipated, Debbie and I found ourselves facing another time of transition and trust.

It was during this time that the Assembly of God in Strasburg, Colorado needed a pastor. This rural community is located forty miles east of Denver in an area known as the "High Plains" (because the altitude is actually higher than Denver). It happened to be the home of my father's family, and where my parents lived when I was born. The towns of Bennett, Strasburg and Byers were located six miles apart because that was the distance you could comfortably travel by horseback or in a wagon in early days. I had relatives who had history and family connections in all three communities.

As a child we would often travel to the area to visit relatives and at times stop for a service at the little Assembly of God that met, in those days, in the old town pool hall. My parents attended this church in their early years of marriage and my father had served as the church treasurer. I have a faint memory of being in a service in the old pool hall as a preteen with the distinct impression that I would serve as the pastor of this church some day.

Debbie and I began to discuss possibilities and I submitted an application to be considered as the new pastor. The church was located on the west end of town in a building built by the congregation and a former pastor. It was on three acres of ground with a doublewide modular behind the church, which served as the pastor's residence. During my college days, I had actually spoken at the church on a Mother's Day. Debbie was with me on that occasion and still had memories of that visit. Those were not fond memories, so she did not possess a sense of anticipation about our future.

We did receive a call from the few members who attended the church to serve as their next senior pastor. My first Sunday was on Labor Day weekend 1982. I was twenty-eight and the oldest and most experienced of the three pastors in town. Lakewood First Assembly was gracious in their support in sending us off to our new venture by providing me with a new desk and office furniture and equipment and a generous offering.

We began the work at our first church knowing we had our work cut out for us. Before my first Sunday, I recall asking my local denominational official about the church. He was honest in his assessment. He said, "Ken, you are going in as the third pastor in a twelve-month period. There are a couple of people in the church who would like to take over if they could. No one has been able to get much accomplished, but who knows? Maybe you can."

With that encouragement, we headed off to our first assignment. I'm sure Debbie's mom shed a few tears when she saw the "house" where her daughter and two young grandchildren would live. We jumped in with the physical and spiritual work that was needed in the church and community. That included work on the church building and the "parsonage." Debbie's father came out and plied his concrete background in pouring new steps for our house. My father installed a fence around the front yard so the children would have a safe place to play and to contain our dogs. I'm sure the experience brought back some memories for my dad. He had installed fences around several small houses in the town over thirty years ago that had been built by his uncle.

We had a local community member help us with mowing and cultivating a garden space that had filled with weeds. Debbie made the comment to him that we were "working and committed to get 'the place in shape,'" to which he responded, "That's what the last three preachers have said!" Did I mention we knew we had our work cut out for us?

We did spend seven years in Strasburg. During that time, we saw the church stabilize financially, numerically and its impact on the community. Mothers of Preschoolers (MOPS) was a new effort in the early to mid-1980's; Debbie, with the help of friend Elaine Drake, the pastor's wife from the Presbyterian church, started a community-wide MOPS group that became one of the largest in the state at the time.

In my desire to make an impact on the community based on my background, I became a nominee in the election for the local Parks and Recreation District Board. I won that election and before completing my term, the opportunity I had in mind came available unexpectedly: a position on the local School Board. As a small rural, unincorporated community the schools were the center of activity and concern. In the spring of 1985, I was elected to the School Board by a margin of three votes. I won over the former Superintendent of Schools and the President of the School Accountability Committee. It was during this time I noticed many State Legislators had backgrounds as School Board members.

While I was the pastor of the church in Strasburg, I recall taking a trip through western Kansas and stopping into see our friends Dr. Bruce and Dovie Gross. He was a family physician in Goodland, Kansas. While we were there, I recall taking a jog by myself. I stood in a wheat field on the edge of town and felt the warm western Kansas breeze and a "voice" or a sense that I would be a pastor in Kansas. At the time I wanted to rebuke that impression, because I couldn't believe it was from the Lord. My impression of that part of Kansas was wrought with some doctrinal teachings with which I didn't agree.

The time was coming for the next School Board election, and my current term was up. My name had been submitted for re-election. At the same time a minister friend named Jack Strom stopped to see me as he traveled through town on his way to Denver. He had a son who was on staff at a church in Colby, Kansas. John Lindell, the Senior Pastor of the church, had resigned to start a new church in a high growth area of Kansas City. The church was a strong, well-attended church and Jack thought I would be a "good fit."

Debbie and I began to pray and discuss this opportunity. I submitted a resume to the search committee and had a few phone interviews. We began to take the opportunity seriously. I recall sitting with our elementary-age children at our favorite Mexican food restaurant in Aurora, and asking them how they would like to move to another town and church. That is one of those conversations I believe they still remember to this day.

All of this created some real conflicts with the timing of a potential move and the School Board election. It looked like a move was in the works. I recall slipping from a sanctuary filled with children from the community attending a kids crusade at our church, to go to the school where a candidate forum took place. I not only slipped in late, but then surprised the group by not telling them why, but asking them to *not* vote for me.

In the coming weeks we experienced another transition. I received one hundred percent of the membership's vote to serve as the next pastor of College Drive Assembly in Colby, Kansas. We felt that was a clear sign of direction from the Lord and for the first time in my life and in Debbie's we would live more than fifty miles from Denver.

Colby, Kansas is known as the "oasis" of Western Kansas. It is a good community. It had a community college, a hospital, two nursing homes, a vibrant and growing business community, a strong agriculture center and about nineteen churches of more varieties than I had ever been exposed to. Compared to Strasburg it was a "legitimate" town, with the familiar agricultural foundation. Debbie taught nursing at the local community college. In addition to my pastoral duties, I found a connection with the local Rotary Club and the Community College baseball team where I helped as a volunteer coach.

We had only been in Colby a year when I received a call from my friend and mentor James Majeske. He asked if I would be available to come speak for him on an upcoming Sunday. I was shocked and honored at the same time. He went on to inform me he considered accepting the position of senior pastor at a large church in Fremont, California. He did want to see if I would be open to being his replacement back in Lakewood. My first thoughts were, *I've only been here one year, and I'm not sure if I want to follow in the 'shoes' of James Majeske!*

Even though we declined to be considered, within a year we heard from some friends that "things weren't going well" with the church in Lakewood. Because of my past connection with the church, and almost nine years as a senior pastor, I felt perhaps this was a situation where I could help. So, we started the process of submitting a resume to the search committee and asking for their consideration.

Once again we found ourselves in the challenging situation of determining the Lord's will and timing. We were called to trust the Lord and discern His direction in the midst of all kinds of cognitive, emotional and spiritual considerations.

We did find the state of the church to be challenging as we entered into the process of being a candidate and deciding what to do. At the same time we were close to the Christmas season and I had the lead role in a drama that was coupled with our "Singing Christmas Tree" presentation. This was a community-wide event held in the Community College Theater. So I felt the stress of the production as well as our decision process.

We went through an arduous series of meetings and services as part of the candidate process. In the final analysis we received enough votes to serve, but it wasn't anywhere close to the one hundred percent we received when we went to our current church. The Lord prepared to us to learn a new level of trust and confidence that comes when we find ourselves in a situation that we know is beyond our human abilities or leadership aptitude.

In January of 1992, I found myself returning to Lakewood First Assembly as their new senior pastor. Once again, I found myself "returning." I returned to my old high school as a teacher; I returned to pastor in the town I lived in when I was born and I returned to serve the church that helped launch me into full-time ministry and my own pastoral ministry career. By the time I ended my pastoral term of service, over fourteen years later, I would return to political service that had its start twenty years prior.

I came to the church with two goals in mind. I wanted to restore consistency of pastoral leadership and to lead the church in addressing relocation plans that were discussed from my time as a staff member in the late 1970's. I am pleased we were able to address the relocation issue through selling our current Lakewood building to Colorado Christian University and purchasing the Foothills Bible Church building on West Belleview near Simms in south Jefferson County.

It is interesting how many leadership lessons are learned when "things don't go well" and I had plenty of opportunities to learn. When I think of some past years, the adage comes to mind, "if I could do it all over again, I wouldn't!" I at least wouldn't do it the same way. What is important is to know the faithfulness of the Lord in *all* circumstances and perfection is not required for progress.

One of the most significant personal times for me spiritually during our relocation project came during a time of worship and prayer at the end of a church service. I felt overwhelmed by the task before us and sensing my inadequacies and stress from many directions. It felt like I could hear the words in my mind and heart that said, *"My presence will go with you and I will give you rest"* (Exodus 33:14, NIV).

This statement is found in the Bible passage when the Lord is speaking to Moses as he prepared to lead God's people to the Promised Land. Moses was overwhelmed with the task that was before him and the Lord spoke words of reassurance of His presence and peace that would accompany Moses as he obeyed and depended upon the Lord.

What is of interest is that verse was "given to me" by a minister by the name of Dick Mills in 1969. Dick Mills had memorized over 700 promises in the Bible. He had a unique ministry in which he would give a scripture of promise from the Bible to people as he felt directed by the Lord. In one service when he was a guest at my home church, he called the teenagers to come forward. To be honest, it appeared many of the verses were somewhat generic, but when he took my hand, he paused and said, *"The Lord says, 'My presence will go with you and I will give you rest.'"* At the time it sounded odd, but I had always remembered that event and that verse from Exodus.

Now I stood before a congregation of people having my own "Moses kind of moment." I asked the Lord "Is this it? Is this the time for that verse spoken almost thirty years ago to a young teenager to come to pass?" From that moment, I knew we would be successful, not because of me, but in spite of me and because of the Lord's faithfulness and promises.

The experiences of life prepare us for each challenge and test life brings. As Debbie and I faced a new phase of life in 2013, the experiences of the past and the lessons learned would once again serve as a guide for what the future would hold. We didn't realize how intense and how soon that would be.

*Chapter 3*

# Facing the Anticipated and the Unanticipated

A s the pages on the calendar turned to 2013, I focused my attention on my work as the Executive Director of Teen Challenge of the Rocky Mountains. I had served as the Executive Director of this faith-based residential drug and alcohol recovery program while serving in the Colorado House. My legislative duties and campaign schedule only allowed me to devote part time to this nonprofit, which is part of a national network of related agencies, known as Teen Challenge USA. Teen Challenge has its roots in the work of Rev. David Wilkerson among heroin addicts and gang members in New York City dating back to the mid-1950's.

In the last six years Teen Challenge of the Rocky Mountains had made consistent progress, primarily due to the day-to-day leadership of my Deputy Director, Gina Brummett. We had just moved our administrative offices to a new space. I anticipated being more involved in day-to-day operations and facilitating some expansion plans for the organization.

Within the first few months of the year, I learned the renters of the house we owned in Fort Collins would be moving at the end of their lease in May. When Debbie's father passed away in 1998, her mother bought a new home in a growing area of southeast Fort Collins. She was the first owner of a newly constructed spacious ranch style house. Over the years when we would visit, Debbie and I commented we could see ourselves living in this house at some point in the future. So, when Debbie's mother passed away in 2011, we purchased the home in anticipation for retirement at some future date.

We had felt fortunate to have good renters for the past two years. I recall sitting with Debbie over lunch in a local Chick-fil-A restaurant and making the statement, "This may be the time for us to consider a move to Fort Collins." I was no longer tied to the Lakewood area by virtue of my elected office and I felt I could continue my Teen Challenge duties as a commuter back to Denver and work on expanding our connections and support in northern Colorado. I believe my statement to Debbie was, "We can roll the dice on continuing to get good renters for the house, or since this is where our future lies, we could go ahead and move at this time."

In July of 2012 Debbie had made a move to join a new hospice organization. Halcyon Hospice has its headquarters in Mead, Colorado although they serve the Front Range of Colorado. When Debbie interviewed for her position, she mentioned we might be moving to Fort Collins "someday" and asked if that would be a problem. They assured her it would be possible for her to transfer to the north team from the south team when that time came. We didn't anticipate the future "someday" coming one year to the day that she began her work with the company.

As we considered all the circumstances, it felt like it was good timing for us to make an "earlier than anticipated move" to Fort Collins and to continue our individual careers from a new city. We spent several months in the transition process. As the activity picked up to prepare for the move, it provided a renewed sense of clarity and anticipation for a future that was muddied with an election loss the previous November. I made several trips to work on the house and to oversee work that we had done before our move. My son and his family would move into our house in Lakewood, so the move could be made more gradually with less stress than what normally accompanies this kind of change in life.

Our moving day was June 30, 2013. Debbie's first day on her new Northern Colorado team with Halcyon Hospice began on July 1, 2013. She didn't have much time off to make the move and settle in, but with the work we had done leading up to the "big move," we felt we could gradually get boxes unloaded and everything set up that wasn't ready, like the master bedroom.

With the Fourth of July holiday, Debbie's work adjustment and my becoming a commuter for my work with Teen Challenge the next two weeks went by quickly. Before long, I faced the week of my quarterly Teen Challenge Board meeting on Friday, July 19, 2013. This meeting was near Salt Lake City in Tooele, Utah where our program for teen girls was located. At the time, Matt and Heather Shaw served as the Directors of New Hope House. The program showed marked progress and there were some improvements to the facility that we all looked forward to seeing.

Our plans were to catch an early flight from Denver to Salt Lake City, drive to the New Hope House facility, have lunch, receive an update on the program, tour the facility, conduct a Board meeting and then catch an evening flight back to Denver. The night before the trip I didn't feel up to par and Debbie was concerned about how I would do. I assured her I would be okay.

The trip from Denver to Salt Lake City went well. Gina Brummett our Deputy Director was on the same flight as was her husband Jim and Pastor Loren Popineau two of our Board members. So I was glad I didn't have to fly alone. It felt like the day went well, but I did notice during lunch that my appetite wasn't that good. (I had lunch with my friends Doug and Pat Powell on Thursday before my Friday meeting; they told me after that lunch, they had commented to each other, "Ken doesn't look well.")

As we moved to the "living room" of the facility, we sat on some couches and heard the ministry reports and conducted some of our business. It was during that time I began to experience a severe head-ache and chills. I sat with the group with blankets wrapped around me trying to keep warm in the middle of July.

My friends gave me some good-natured ribbing about me being "contagious" and not wanting to sit next to me on the plane ride home. I don't get sick often and was sure the symptoms would be short lived. My friend Jim Brummett was concerned about how I was doing and even offered to drive me back home to Fort Collins. I assured him that I thought I would be okay. I slept most of the flight back to Denver and tried to get to my car as quickly as possible when we arrived in Denver, so I could get home to Fort Collins. I did call Jim to let him know I had made it safely home.

It was good to get some sleep in my own home, even if we still slept in our guest bedroom, not having set up the master bedroom. Saturday morning, Debbie's sister, Sue Schmidt and her cousin, Cheryl Pierson came over for a morning breakfast on the patio. I joined the "breakfast with the gals" for a brief time, but didn't have much of an appetite. I didn't realize at the time that would be the one of the last meals of solid food I would eat for almost two months.

My symptoms continued with only some periodic relief. Since it was the weekend, we found a "minor emergency" clinic that was open on weekends. I drove myself to an appointment. The nurse practitioner took vital signs and did some blood work, but couldn't find anything definitive. I found myself returning to the clinic on Sunday, but now I needed Debbie to drive me. The nurse practitioner told us that we needed to get in to see our primary care doctor first thing on Monday. Having just moved to Fort Collins and a history of seeing a family physician only every two or three years for some minor seasonal sickness, connecting with a new primary care doctor had not been a priority.

I was at the end of the season for my senior softball team and the tournament would be coming up soon. Also, Debbie and I had made reservations to attend the Western Conservative Summit. Since we were now in Fort Collins, we had made hotel reservations to be able to participate in the full conference without the conflict of legislative duties. So, I knew I had to get better soon. We were able to get in late on Monday afternoon, July 22, 2013 with Dr. Steve Sunderman. We had never met Dr. Sunderman, so he took us on "blind" with little understanding about my medical history while I faced a major health crisis.

Dr. Sunderman is a seasoned physician and approaches his work professionally, wearing a suit and tie with a stethoscope around his neck. We were fortunate that the clinic had a "high ops" room for patients like me. I found myself in this room awaiting tests results while IV fluids were administered. I had a fever of 103 degrees that held steady and at times escalated.

Dr. Sunderman finally came in and told me that he could not determine what was "going on" and thought I should go to the hospital. I tried to reassure him that I would be okay. Because of my urinary issues, Debbie had him insert a catheter to help with my urinary retention. That was "one of those procedures" I hoped I would never need. I didn't realize it would be a permanent fixture over the next four months. Dr. Sunderman consented to let me go home (probably since Debbie was a nurse) but made me promise "If Debbie says during the night that it was time to go to the hospital," I wouldn't argue with her.

I was glad to get home to familiar surroundings and to try to get some much-needed rest. I was confident I would be better in the morning; however, within an hour I began to have vomiting episodes. Debbie was concerned it looked like blood. So, off to the hospital we went near midnight, only to find the emergency room was unusually busy. I sat in a wheelchair with my plastic pan in my lap, feeling miserable. We were finally processed to go to a room in the emergency unit. Being in the waiting emergency waiting room is all that I would recall for several weeks. The experience for Debbie and my family would be far different as they came to my bedside. They did not know what was happening or what the future would hold and certainly were not prepared for what I would experience and the journey they would share with me for almost five months before I returned home.

*Chapter 4*

# The Long Campaign Begins

P olitical campaigns are interesting endeavors in many ways. They are long, arduous and come more quickly than you realize, especially for a two-year term. They require a lot of hard work, strategies, time, cooperation, and support from volunteers and donors. Often that support comes from unexpected places. The outcome for many campaigns is dependent on many factors that you don't have control over and the timing of the election and certain events can make all the difference.

I was surprised how much these elements would be a part of my life as I began to wage a different kind of "campaign." I was not involved in a battle for political survival, but in a battle for my physical survival. This campaign would not only be matter of a "season" or months, but would continue for over two years. I also realized how much the experiences of the past prepare you for the challenges of the future.

After being admitted to the emergency room on July 22, 2013, I was finally taken to an ICU room around 5:00 the next morning. The high fever already had an impact on my mind and emotions. Debbie told me that I made the statement to the doctors, "Release me or get me to a regular room!"

I discovered one of the greatest challenges you can face in medical care is the mind numbing, miserable hours in an emergency room. In the summer of 2012, the Colorado Medical Society had honored me with their highest recognition. It is called the "Protector of the Patient" Award, but now for the first time in my life since birth, and after years visiting hospitals as a pastor, I was in a hospital, as a patient.

I was finally transferred to a regular medical unit in the hospital as they ran tests. At this point the diagnosis was a "high fever of unknown origin." They ran blood tests, followed by a spinal tap. Finally, on Thursday Debbie was informed my diagnosis was encephalitis caused by West Nile Virus. Only one percent of West Nile infections result in the most serious "neuro-invasive" form and of those only one percent of the cases are accompanied by encephalitis or meningitis. I was diagnosed with both.

During these initial days my family quickly rallied to my bedside. My daughter Stephanie flew in from Atlanta with their youngest daughter, Mckenzie, who was seven months old. Five months earlier Mckenzie was in the hospital as a newborn with RSV and Rhino Virus. My son Christian adjusted his work schedule and came up to Loveland from Lakewood. When he was a Missionary Associate on Leyte Island in the Philippines, he contracted Dengue Fever, a mosquito-borne disease. Christian was in a third world hospital for several days recovering from that experience. I'm sure what I went through, especially with the diagnosis, brought back some memories.

West Nile disease is a viral infection that is spread to people by bites from infected mosquitoes. Symptoms can range from none at all to severe illness. About seventy-five percent of people who are infected are asymptomatic and about twenty-five percent will develop West Nile fever. Less than one percent develops the more severe neuro-invasive form, which can lead to hospitalization, critical illness, chronic disability or even death.

It was surprising for me to learn mosquito-borne disease is the cause for the greatest amount of health issues worldwide. According to the American Mosquito Control Association, "Mosquitoes cause more human suffering than any other organism — over one million people worldwide die from mosquito-borne diseases every year"

Both humans and animals are affected. When I attended the Western Conservative Summit in 2014, I remember seeing a bald eagle that had suffered a West Nile disease disability. I also recall meeting a member of Timberline Church in Fort Collins, who was involved in research at Colorado State University on the effect of West Nile Virus on horses.

West Nile Virus was first detected in New York in 1999 and began to spread rapidly to 2002, showing up in forty-four states. The virus is carried by the culex mosquito and is spread when infected birds migrate and are bitten by mosquitoes, which in turn infect humans and animals.

In Colorado, West Nile Virus is found in high concentrations in Larimer and Weld Counties. In 2013, forty-eight percent of the pools of water that were confirmed as having West Nile mosquitoes were found in Larimer County. Of the reported West Nile Virus cases almost 30 percent of those infected in Colorado lived in Larimer County.

The word of my illness and hospitalization spread rapidly. The Denver news stations and several media outlets contained stories about one of the first reported cases of West Nile Virus in 2013 affecting "Former State Representative Ken Summers." One of the first friends to contact my family and send flowers was State Senator Andy Kerr, who had defeated me in the 2012 election nine months earlier.

The hospital staff encouraged Debbie to prepare for my discharge soon after my diagnosis. My daughter Stephanie spent the night with me as I closed in on my first week of hospitalization. Early in the morning on July 30, 2013 the nurse came into my room and warned her that in a few minutes, there would be a lot of staff members in the room and "they needed to call her mother right away"! She told them that Debbie was on her way and she would meet her in the hospital lobby. All she could communicate to Debbie when she arrived was, "Dad is crashing!" The virus and brain trauma had affected my muscles and respiratory system causing respiratory failure. They rushed me to ICU and began life-saving measures including placing me on a respirator. In coming days they would insert a feeding tube to provide the nourishment I would receive for several weeks. They eventually performed a tracheotomy to provide ongoing repository support. I wouldn't come off of life support until six weeks later.

Within my first few days in the intensive care unit, I received a visit from three of my legislative colleagues. Senator Jerry Sonnenberg, Senator Kevin Lundberg and Senator Ted Harvey, had not only served with me at the Capitol, but also attended a weekly Bible study with me at the Capitol. These three came not to only check up on me and encourage me in my recovery, but to pray. Also former State Representative Jim Welker from Loveland made several visits to monitor my progress and offer his prayers. Many family members and friends would follow, including Representative Frank

McNulty the Speaker of the House during my last term. The time and effort of these and many others who traveled great distances for a few minutes was truly humbling.

The encephalitis had impacted my ability to speak. It so happened that the COO of McKee Hospital in Loveland had an Occupational Therapy background. She would come into my room late at night after making her final rounds for a visit. She was able to "read my lips" so we could communicate. My family reports the conversations were fairly extensive considering my condition and covered a variety of topics from my legislative experience to health care issues. I'm sure the stimulation was good for my eventual cognitive recovery, which was in question for much of the time. Most of my communication was with a laminated page of symbols and the alphabet. I used it to point to pictures and spell out words to communicate my needs; often to the frustration of others and myself.

I would spend twenty-two days in ICU before being transferred to the Northern Colorado Acute Care Hospital. The goal was for me to gain the strength and recovery needed to face an unexpected surgery.

The need for surgery arose from an issue discovered in my early days of hospitalization. Doctor Anthony Pierson, the Hospitalist at McKee Hospital, was concerned there was more to be diagnosed. He insisted my neurologist conduct a CT-scan of my chest. While they did so reluctantly, what they found surprised them. I had a tumor in my chest and the presence of a thymus gland indicated I also had a rare neuromuscular disorder known as Myasthenia Gravis. This contributed to my health crisis by depleting my immune system. My good antibodies were "fighting each other" so I could not stave off any infections. So, with my respiratory failure, I battled ongoing pneumonia and a deterioration of my muscle mass that resulted in a forty pound weight loss and the need of a "dialysis-like" process known as plasmapharesis. The procedure took several hours over several days and essentially replaced all my antibodies with new ones in hopes to strengthen my immune system.

During this time, the toll of being confined to a bed on life support was more intense than I could have anticipated. Debbie and Christians had conversations expressing concerns that I had "given up." They realized I wanted to see some signs of hope and progress and kept talking to me about the next steps and how that would help. The one saving grace was the medication I received that kept me sedated and created a state of amnesia.

Also, recovering from brain trauma was a challenging experience. My emotions were difficult to manage and staying alert was a challenge. Headaches, confusion, a serious bed wound and gaining a sense of orientation to time proved to be a struggle for weeks. When nursing staff appeared insensitive to my condition and needs, it compounded the anxiety and created more of a struggle.

When I moved to the Northern Colorado Acute Care Hospital, it was in hopes that I would soon be able to return to McKee Hospital to have the "thymectomy" surgery that would remove the tumor and my thymus gland. This surgery was viewed as a step to address the Myasthenia Gravis and was the key procedure to get me up and on the road to full recovery, hopefully within a year.

I began having occupational, physical and respiratory and speech therapy along with all the high level nursing care my condition required. For weeks I was a "total care" patient. My case was also followed by a team of physicians, which included the hospital Medical Director, neurologist, infectious disease doctor and pulmonologist along with the general surgeon.

Debbie was in constant communication with the surgeon. The scheduled date for the surgery was delayed and then delayed again. When you are recovering from complete paralysis and still dependent upon others for your care, a week's delay can feel like an eternity. I felt like I experienced one crisis or issue after another.

One of those crises took place in the middle of the night as a nurse and assistant tested the contents of my stomach from the nourishment I received from a feeding tube. In the process, air was introduced that caused spontaneous vomiting. At the time I was more asleep than awake, I remember the nursing assistant saying, "He is throwing up!" They quickly raised my head, but it was too late to avoid the aspiration that we had worked so hard to avoid. The next day when Debbie showed up, I began to realize the seriousness of what had happened. The reality set in and I realized this had caused another delay in the surgery schedule.

While in this "waiting with anticipation" mode, the general surgeon came to my room and surprised me by saying, "We are perplexed and we need your input as to what to do." He went on to explain the infection in my lungs was severe and they were not sure if it could be cleared. He presented the option of waiting another month and treating it aggressively with more antibiotics or they could remove the lower lob of my left lung.

As we discussed the options and what each of them meant, it appeared removing the portion of my lung was the best option. He explained the exchange between the oxygen from my lung to the blood stream was so hampered that it kept me in a weakened condition. He said the physician team overseeing my case would meet the next day to discuss the options. I recall asking for prayer that this team would have clarity and unity in what was best.

While we waited for the final decision, good news did come our way. On September 17, Dr. Brent Peters, my pulmonologist, came into the room and announced, "Ken, this is a big day for you; you are officially off of life-support." I recall the first thought that came to mind was, *I've been on life support!* In the midst of my traumatic brain injury I knew my condition was serious, but we had not talked about "life support" in those words. In total I was on a "life support" for seven weeks.

The surgery was finally scheduled and I adopted a "no more crises" theme until that time. To help with that, Debbie arranged for some friends to come spend the entire night with me. This was for them to help with my issues during the night and call the nurse if needed and to "protect" me at times from the staff. The dedication of these friends, many who traveled from Denver to be with me, was greatly appreciated and humbling.

I was moved from the high observation room to a "regular" room in the acute hospital for the final days leading up to the day of surgery. I encountered an unexpected challenge. If I laid on my right side, the fluid from my left lung would move into my throat and begin to choke me. There were several times this occurred not only creating the sensation of "choking to death" but requiring Debbie (who fortunately was close by) to quickly open the passage way of my trach hardware to allow me to breathe.

My surgery took place on Thursday, September 26, 2013, a little over two months after my initial hospitalization. Normally the removal of the thymus gland is done through the middle of the chest, much like a heart surgery. The surgeons attempted to do two surgeries at one time. One surgeon removed the lower lobe of my left lung while the other removed the tumor in my chest and the thymus gland. So they made the decision to perform the surgeries by an incision on my left side. They removed the infected portion of my lung and then came across to the center of my chest to remove the tumor and the thymus gland.

The surgery was challenging more than I realized. I tried to ignore the risks involved, but remember giving Debbie the names of some pallbearers, "just in case." The surgery proved to be a success and I recall the sense of relief and satisfaction in Dr. Tulis' mood after his post-surgery visit.

I spent two weeks at McKee Hospital for the post-surgery recovery period. I had a number of drainage tubes coming out of my left side. One of the drains was not successful in removing collected fluids. As a result, I had a large hematoma on my left side that bulged out from my visible ribs. Several weeks later, while in the Northern Colorado Rehabilitation Hospital, the hematoma burst, creating quite a panic among the staff. . The wound specialist attached a drainage bag to my side to catch the fluids that continued to drain for several days.

I returned to Northern Colorado Acute Care Hospital, but was there only a few days before being transferred to the rehabilitation hospital. Fortunately this meant taking a trip down the hall to a different section of the building. I experienced three transfers in five days. Those types of adjustments are not usually that challenging, but for someone still recovering from a traumatic brain injury and major surgery, it presented more of an emotional and mental challenge than I expected.

During my time in the Acute Care Hospital, Debbie kept me focused and motivated by telling me that as I improved, I would be able to "go through the double doors" that separated the acute care hospital from the rehabilitation hospital. I told her, "I guess that's better than going through the pearly gates."

The staff joined together and lined the hall leading to the rehabilitation hospital with the song "Happy Trails to You" playing in the background. This was their way to celebrate my progress that allowed me to move forward with my recovery. I had spent forty days in the acute care hospital and Debbie and I had become well acquainted with all of the staff.

I would spend sixty days in the rehabilitation hospital, with physical and occupational therapy three hours each day. That time would be filled with progress and challenges. Sometimes, three steps forward and two steps back. I was finally able, still with assistance, to stand and walk between the parallel bars in the therapy gym. Before my surgery, my feeding tube was removed and I gradually was able to take in a regular diet. This was a gradual process, constantly aware of aspiration risks. I faced the dual challenge of needing to eat to regain weight and strength, but not having much of an appetite in spite of being sustained by a feeding tube for weeks.

In anticipation of my return home, an evaluation was made of the suitability of our home to accommodate my needs. We had a ramp and grab bars installed and some doors fitted with hinges that widened the door openings to accommodate my wheelchair.

Another part of the preparation for returning home included a couple of "community outings." These were trips supervised by therapists to help me acclimate to life outside the hospital. One of those trips was to a staff meeting at Timberline Church. It provided an opportunity for me to thank them for their support and share my progress.

On December 10, 2013, the loud speaker at Northern Colorado Rehabilitation Hospital announced, "Code Ken." This was a signal to staff that I was leaving the hospital for home. Several friends and family members gathered for the occasion and about 100 staff members that included doctors, nurses, housekeeping, maintenance workers, cooks and administrators lined the hallway to send me off. I had been a "resident" in the two hospital units at Northern Colorado Rehabilitation and Acute Care Hospital for 100 days. I took the opportunity to give a "speech" to thank everyone for their care and contribution to my progress and to encourage them in their work.

I returned home to celebrate the upcoming Christmas holidays with family and was pleased to be back to the home where I had lived less than a month before being admitted to the hospital. After our move on June 30, 2013, I spent the first night in my own bed in our master bedroom on December 10, 2013. The next phase was to adjust to life at home and continue with home rehabilitation. What we would find was the path ahead would not be as clear-cut as anticipated. The long campaign would continue in some unexpected ways.

## Chapter 5

# Detours on the Road to Recovery

W hen I returned home, I was greeted with a new piece of furniture. The members of the Colorado House donated money
to purchase a new therapeutic recliner. Former Speaker of the House
Frank McNulty was a constant source of support and kept in touch
with Debbie about my needs. He led the effort to ensure I was fully
prepared for my return home. Representative John Becker, whom
I served with in the House, had family in the furniture business
and arranged for the chair purchase and even for the delivery. This
would be the only chair I would use outside of my wheelchair. When
I returned home, I was dependent on a power wheelchair and on
Debbie for transferring me from the wheelchair to my new chair.

I arrived home on a Tuesday and began the next phase of my
recovery the next day. I had an assessment visit from my home
physical therapist and returned to my primary care physician for
my post-hospital follow-up. My physical therapist, Kelly Schilling,
suggested what sounded like an aggressive and almost impossible
goal. He put out the challenge that I would be able to use a walker
to get from the bathroom door to the toilet or shower bench within a

month. Since I couldn't stand and had not taken a step with a walker, navigating six feet felt like a walk around the block.

Before leaving the rehabilitation hospital, I had just finished IV antibiotic treatments for an infection. So, Dr. Sunderman did urine and blood tests on Wednesday during my post-hospital visit. On Friday, we would return for a follow up appointment.

We were pleased our long-time friends Tom and Judy Price from Ohio were in Fort Collins for a visit. When Friday arrived we had a planned dinner with them and Debbie's sister and brother-in-law, Sue and Sam Schmidt. Also, my son Christian and his family joined us for a "pre-Christmas" coming home celebration.

We left our company to go to my doctor's appointment. We sat in Dr. Sunderman's office as he carefully reviewed lab results. We were eager to get the appointment finished and get home in time to enjoy a Friday evening with our family and friends and continue the celebration of being home from the hospital. Dr. Sunderman commented about the elevated white blood count and came to the conclusion that it would be best to have the infectious disease doctors "make the call on treatment." As a result, he said I needed to return to McKee Hospital and he would make the call to let them know I would be on my way.

As we left the appointment, we began to process the disappointing news; our hearts sank and the emotions of what we faced set in. We didn't feel a sense of urgency, so we went home tried to enjoy the meal with our guests and had the grandchildren open some early Christmas presents. Later that evening, we made the trip to McKee Hospital. Our friends Tom and Judy would accompany us and spend several hours of waiting during the emergency room vigil. I was finally admitted and treated for an infection and released the following Monday. I found myself leaving a hospital twice within a seven-day period. When I returned home, I continue my recovery with self-administered IV antibiotics for several weeks.

In two weeks, we would enjoy Christmas with our children and grandchildren thankful I was at home and we were all together. We had survived the past five months with all of its challenges, together. The week of Christmas, our friends and photographers Glen and Mary Janssen came to Fort Collins to take some family pictures. It was a great way to celebrate my homecoming and a future filled with anticipation of better days.

As the New Year dawned, I focused on my home physical and occupational therapy. I recall taking my first difficult two steps with a walker and being exhausted after the effort. However, the seemingly impossible goal of navigating from the bathroom door to the toilet and shower was achieved within the time limit goal that was set one month earlier. I think Kelly had tears in his eyes as it happened.

I learned how to adjust to my need for rest as the Myasthenia Gravis symptoms continued to manifest. The disorder creates weakness and fatigue but with rest allows for strength to be regenerated. On Friday night, February 21, 2014, Debbie and I got out for a rare venture away from home and ran a few errands and then had dinner at Red Robin, one of our favorite restaurants. When I came home, I felt the familiar sense of fatigue and even though it was 5:00 p.m., I laid down for a nap.

When I woke up an hour later, I had the strange sensation of feeling rested but not feeling well. I still got up and worked on writing my daily blog. As I wrote, I reflected on signs of progress from the past several weeks. At the same time I sensed my fragile condition and at the end of the blog, asked people to pray—right now! I had a severe headache. Debbie took my temperature, which was over 100 and continued to rise. She treated me the best she could and even suggested, "We should go to the emergency room." That thought was more painful than my symptoms so, I went to bed anticipating feeling better in the morning. The night was rough with restlessness and vomiting, but I was finally able to get some sleep.

"Ken, Ken! Can you hear me?!" I could hear Debbie's voice and feel her hand pushing on my arm, but I could not respond. On Saturday morning, Debbie needed to help me transfer from the bed to my wheelchair. I made it out to the kitchen table, but that was it, before slipping into a semi-conscious state.

Debbie called 911. When the paramedics arrived, my blood pressure was 60 over 0. They looked at Debbie and asked, *"How aggressive are we to be?"* I tell people that I'm glad she didn't have to think about her response!

Because of my critical condition, I was rushed me to Poudre Valley Hospital in Fort Collins as the closest medical facility. The hospital had just completed an intensive training on treating septic shock and I was the first patient to arrive for them to put into practice their new training and procedures.

I was admitted to the ICU and responded quickly to the treatment. After two days in ICU I was transferred to a regular hospital room. The tests revealed I had an abscess on my left kidney that spawned an infection that went into my blood stream and urinary system. The infection also impacted my heart function. I was surprised when I received a visit from a nurse educator who said she was visiting me to "discuss my congestive heart failure." At first I thought, *She must have the wrong patient.* I was glad this issue was quick to clear up and my heart function returned to normal in a short period of time.

The septic shock episode left me weakened and diminished the recovery I had experienced in the past month. As a result, I was readmitted to Northern Colorado Rehabilitation Hospital for ten days of continued recovery. By the time I returned home, I felt that I not only regained my progress toward recovery, but also made some improvement from two weeks earlier. That enabled me to return home in good condition to continue my home therapy. I eventually made sufficient progress in my home therapy to be able to return to Northern Colorado Rehabilitation Hospital for outpatient therapy.

When I was hospitalized, I recall doctors telling me that most of those who experience severe cases of West Nile Virus recover within a year and return to the full activity and function they had before the infection. I kept my focus on my recovery, anticipating that would be the case for me. However, I faced some ongoing challenges.

It truly was a "three steps forward, two steps back" kind of a year for me in 2014. Every six to eight weeks I encountered a major infection that required hospitalization and IV antibiotics. My situation stumped and concerned my infectious disease doctor. Even with those challenges, I was able to engage in some work projects for a few months from my home office. I also transitioned from home therapy to outpatient therapy at Northern Colorado Rehabilitation Hospital.

My last of four hospitalizations in 2014 took place in August. Within the first six months of 2015, I "graduated" from outpatient rehabilitation and was able to continue my therapy with the help of a trainer at a local fitness center. As I marked the two-year anniversary of my hospitalization, I still found myself in the "recovery" process.

While I am still dependent upon crutches and have weakness in my legs and limited range of motion in my shoulders, I am able to drive a car and have started to return to taking on some contracts as a Governmental Affairs Consultant based on my political experience. From a medical standpoint, doctors and therapists have expressed some doubts as to whether I will experience "full recovery." However, I am confident, with hard work and the Lord's help, the future will be bright.

As I continue my recovery, I find myself still reflecting on the many lessons and observations about my life and experiences from hospital to home. I will share some of those lessons in following chapters. Before I do that, here are some devotional thoughts to consider.

\*\*\*\*\*\*\*\*\*\*\*\*\*\*\*\* \*\*\*\*\*\*\*\*\*\*\*\*\*\*\*\*\*\*\*\* \*\*\*\*\*\*\*\*\*\*\*\*\*\*\*\*\*\*

## When You Find Yourself, Where You Don't Want to Be

**BIBLE VERSE FOR TODAY...** *"Fear not, for I am with you; be not dismayed, for I am your God. I will strengthen you, Yes, I will help you, I will uphold you with My righteous right hand."* (Isaiah 41:10, NKJV)

Over the generations and even millennia, God's people have found themselves "where they didn't want to be." They were slaves in Egypt, defeated by enemies in the Promised Land, judged by the Lord, in captivity by a foreign godless nation, and they faced the struggle of being re-established in their own land. The circumstances of the nation are reflective of individuals in the Bible and even our life today.

Often we find ourselves "where we didn't want to be." Perhaps that is facing the loss of a job, the loss of a marriage, financial bankruptcy, the loss of a loved one, or as in my situation— bed-ridden and disabled by an unexpected and rare health crisis. The list can feel endless.

What I have found, is regardless of how you ended up in "those" types of situations, it doesn't matter the details or circumstances that brought you to that point, the issue is you are there!

It was when God's people were in one of those "circumstances where they did not want to be" that we find some of the most well-known and reassuring words of scripture, *"Fear not, for I am with you; be not dismayed, for I am your God. I will strengthen you, Yes, I will help you, I will uphold you with My righteous right hand"* (Isaiah 41:10, NKJV) What is it that you need to know, that you need to remind yourselves of in "those" types of circumstances? You need to remember:

**The Lord is with you — and He is God!** When we realize the Lord is with us and rely on His awesome power, it drives out fear and confronts our worry about life and the future. We can be reassured of God's care. Jesus said, *"don't worry about these things [food, clothing, shelter]. . . your heavenly Father already knows all your needs"* (Matthew 6:33, NLT). If the Lord can provide the basics and essentials, He can provide all that we need. God's love for us is perfect and *"perfect love drives out all fear"* (1 John 4:18, NIV).

You can take heart because the **Lord is the eternal God and He is not going anywhere!** *"I, the Lord, am the one. I was here at the beginning, and I will be here when all things are finished"* (Isaiah 41:4, NCV).

You need to remember the **Lord's strength and support is being extended to you in your time of need**. It may come through various sources and in various ways. That is what I observed in my many months of illness and prolonged recovery. Sometimes God intervenes sovereignly doing only what He alone can do. At others times, He uses people as His agents of encouragement and help. We see the Apostle Paul alluding to this, *"But God, who encourages those who are discouraged, encouraged us by the arrival of Titus"* (2 Corinthians 7:6, NLT). At another time we see the Lord speaking directly to Paul and saying, *"My grace is sufficient for you, for my power is made perfect in weakness"* (2 Corinthians 12:9, ESV).

**Strength and support**. At times the Lord empowers us to do what we in our own strength cannot and could not otherwise do. At other times, we move forward one step in front of the other, taking each day at a time, being "carried" by the Lord. I think of being in a swimming pool with my grandchildren and them laying back while I support them and carry them along. For me, that is a good imagery of the Lord providing us the support we need as we relax in His care.

What do you do, when you find yourself where you don't want to be? The concepts can sound trite, but remember their power. God is with you. He is providing the strength and support you need as you trust in Him and rest in Him.

Senate campaign announcement 2012

New home, new start July 1, 2013

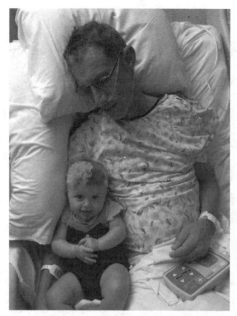

Granddaughter Mckenzie July 29, 2013

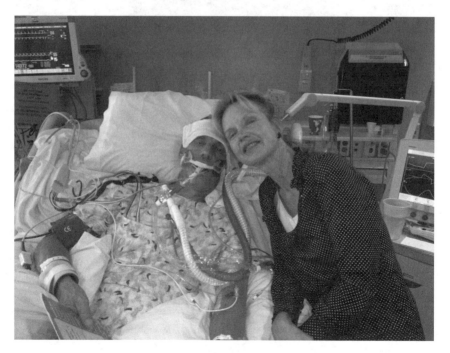

ICU Debbie

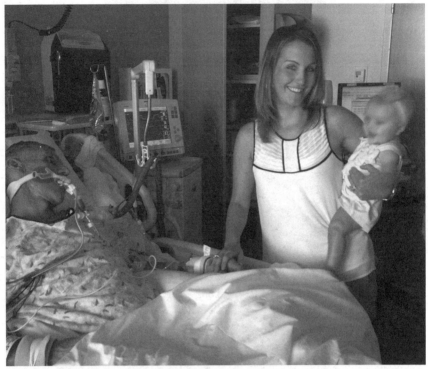

ICI visit Stephanie and Mckenzie

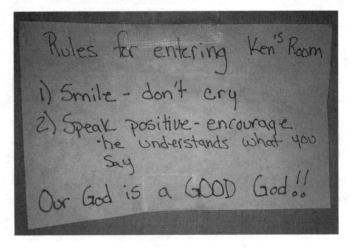

Room Sign

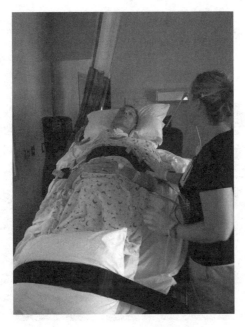

Tilt bed Acute Care Hospital

Family visit Acute Care Hospital

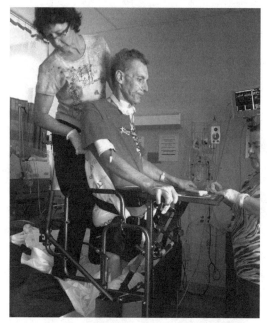

Standing frame

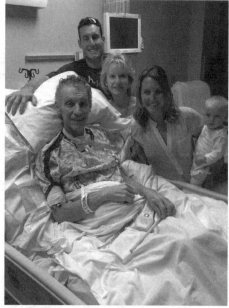

McKee Hospital ready for surgery

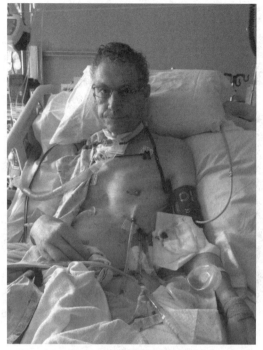

post-surgery drain tubes

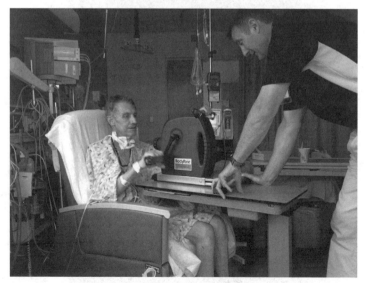

post-surgery therapy

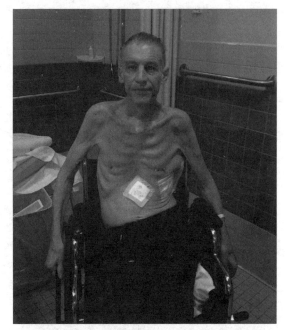

ready to return to Acute Care hospital

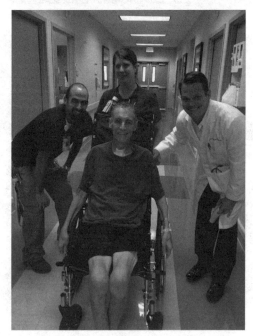

leaving Acute Care for Rehab Hospital

## Chapter 6

# Challenged and Changed

Y ou can count on it. A crisis in life will challenge you and change
you. It will reveal what you do know and don't know about
yourself and it will refine you. Remember, for every "testimony" is
someone who encountered and survived the "test."

What happens when a position, ability or level of status that has
formed one's identity comes to an end? Many have faced the challenge of "life after" they are no longer in the limelight. A legislative
colleague once observed, , "In politics, in a moment of time, you can
go from a 'who's who' to 'who's that?'"

When position, status or abilities that form one's identity is
removed, the foundation of life is revealed. That can happen through
a variety of ways, but none as devastating as a sudden and unexpected illness that threatens life and leaves you totally paralyzed
and dependent upon others. In those moments, status, dignity and
self-sufficiency come to an end.

The question I get asked the most is, "How did you handle all that
you went through?" The observation that people make most often is

related to my positive attitude in the midst of all the challenges that I have faced.

Through my observations of other people, as a pastor and through my own experience, I have found it is true that there are three basic responses to tragedy. Those character-testing times in life will defeat you, define you or make you determined to overcome them.

"Giving up" is a position of hopelessness. Life is viewed as having no future, no meaning and no purpose. My family at times wondered if my resolve weakened. I recall my son reporting during one trying stretch, asking me if I "felt like giving up." I'm glad I responded with, "No." I am reminded of Solomon's words, *"If you faint in the day of adversity, your strength is small"* (Proverbs 24:10, ESV).

Being "defined" by tragedy means you allow circumstances to determine your identity and outlook on life. You begin to view yourself through the lens of your condition or limitations or state in life. The default position is to view yourself as a victim, to be a whiner, and to give into pity.

My friend, Tim Brotzman, has gone through some of the most challenging physical and personal crises I have observed. Multiple rear-end car accidents have left him paralyzed costing him greatly in many ways. I recall a statement Tim mentioned to me at one time that kept coming to my mind as I laid on my back, paralyzed in a hospital bed. He said, "I may have a condition, but my condition does not have me!" What matters is our relationship with God, with family and with others; when we allow relationships to define our life that is an identity that cannot be taken away.

To be "determined" in the face of tragedies requires a strong commitment and focus. It requires a resolve to be a victor, to be a winner and to be powerful. The Apostle James said, *"the testing of your faith produces perseverance"* (James 1:3, NIV). I'm not sure if I considered myself a patient person; however, when you don't have any choice but to wait, it does have an impact on your life, and you learn patience.

Determination in the face of a crisis makes you quick to recognize your limitations.

People often say, "The Lord won't give me more than I can handle." I remind them that is not in the Bible. The Bible does say the Lord will *"not allow you to be* tempted *beyond what you are able"* (1 Corinthians 10:13, NIV). What Jesus said was, *"apart from me, you can do nothing"* (John 15:5, ESV), but through Christ's strength, He will give us the provisions that we need to face each day.

Facing a health crisis leads to self-discovery and self-development. You are never sure what you are prepared to face. All of the things I never wanted to go through, I experienced in a relatively short span of time. What I have observed in others and in myself is, "you don't know what you can go through until you have to go through it."

As I reflect on my life and my illness, I realize my personality and experiences prepared me for what I was to face. I have always been a disciplined and hard worker. In my younger years, I was probably the proverbial "workaholic" and one who was addicted to my own adrenaline. During my legislative years, I was known as one of the hardest working campaigners in the House. As a runner, I kept pushing myself and when I felt I couldn't go any farther, I would say to myself, *"Make it to the end of the next block"*, and then I would push beyond that point.

At the same time, I didn't view myself as needing "to be in charge." I was more motivated by a sense of service and bringing out the best in others and helping others achieve success. I also grew up with an understanding that following God's "call" for my life did not have to be in a specific position or in "full-time" ministry. So whether serving as a teacher, pastor or elected official, I viewed myself as fulfilling God's call on my life. As a result, I believed there are always opportunities for someone dedicated to serve and make a difference.

Each situation an individual faces is unique to them, their life situation, history, personality and the time the crisis occurs. Often I would hear of what others experienced and would view their situation far more challenging than my own.

My illness was not only a test of my "mettle," but also a test for my wife. Debbie has spent her career as a nurse, mother and pastor's wife. She has great leadership skills, but does not seek nor is often willing to accept a leadership role in her work. She knows what motivates her and understands her passion and is comfortable where those two intersect. She has a clear understanding of what she can do and what she feels called to do.

As I was hospitalized, I believe my adult children saw "a side of mom" they didn't realize was there. She assessed situations and made decisions that needed to be made when they needed to be made. That included setting up a Caring Bridge account so the many friends and family members could follow my status. She also made the contacts that were needed to make sure I would be able to be admitted to Northern Colorado Rehabilitation Hospital. She was in constant contact with the surgeon leading up to my surgery and was my advocate and constant companion for twelve to fourteen hours a day, seven days a week for over 140 days of my hospitalization.

The same determination and dedication was reflected in my family. My daughter Stephanie flew in from Atlanta within two days of my hospitalization and was back and forth between Atlanta and Denver at least five times of the next five months. My son Christian and his family "stepped up to the plate" to help however and whenever they could. (I will share more about their perspective in the following chapter.)

When you are on your back, paralyzed for days on life support, it does provide an opportunity for soul searching and reassessment. I often say, "If I had it to do all over again, I wouldn't." During this time I learned more about myself, God and the priorities of life. If I were honest with myself, I would look back on some of my activities and drive and my approach to life and conclude I attempted to prove my worth to myself and others, only to find out they weren't paying attention!

At times Debbie would resign herself to my approach to life with the attitude, "I am prepared for the fact that you might not live that long with the pace of life and the pressure you put on yourself." The reality was most of my stress in life was "self imposed." So, while being on your back in a hospital is not where you want to be, it was a time of forced rest. I experienced the reality of Psalm 23 when it says, *"he makes me lie down"* (Psalm 23:2a, ESV).

Debbie's life as a hospice nurse was as demanding and as hectic as mine. Not only was there the time and emotional demands of caring for patients with a terminal illness, but also there were evenings of endless charting and paper work, along with occasional on-call nights and weekends.

When I went into a crisis at the end of my first week in the hospital, Debbie informed her boss that she had to leave and wasn't sure when she would return. She made the commitment to be by my side to encourage me and fight for my care. This provided an opportunity for us to develop a new dimension of our thirty-seven-year-old marriage. I joke with others, telling them, "I found a brain injury can help your wife have more patience with you."

Often, times of stress and adjustment from a health crisis can tear a relationship apart. I'm glad that was not the case for us. When I was in my hospital bed, I would look across the room where Debbie was and my greatest desire was to get out of bed and go sit with her. I found the best part of my day was when Debbie entered my hospital room and the most difficult part of my day was when she would leave to go home.

As I recently shared my story with someone, they commented, "If you didn't have a strong relationship with the Lord before that experience, I am sure you do now." After being a "lifelong" Christian and serving twenty-eight years in ministry, I did find a renewal in my heart not only in my relationship with the Lord, but an awareness of His mercy, grace and strength that He provides on a daily basis.

My health crisis and prolonged recovery has forced me into a "new normal." I continue to test the limits of my strength and endurance. At times, I find periods of intensive mental activity can be as taxing as physical activity.

I find with some ongoing Myasthenia Gravis symptoms, I can't work as hard for as long as I was used to without becoming overly fatigued. If I push too much, the level of exertion that helps others strengthen muscles actually hinders my muscle development. So, instead of a day of recovery, I need several days to recover and feel back to "normal."

In one conversation I commented, "It feels like I have a built-in governor." For someone who has lived their life going as far as I could, and doing as much as I could and then going a little further and doing a little more, this is an adjustment. However, I am finding my "new normal" is the needed balance for my life.

I have made it a practice to read through the Bible each year for over thirty years. At times it may have been more routine than at others, but I have always made it part of my spiritual discipline. I have found "as you read the Bible, it reads you." I have discovered familiar verses or passages making a new impact depending on where I was in my life or the issues I face. .

I had finished reading through the Bible in 2013, right before my hospitalization. Since coming home from the hospital, I have read through the Bible two times each year. Out of my experience and Bible reading, I began writing a daily devotional that I post on my website, www.kensummers.org.

When I was hospitalized, Debbie began posting a daily status report on my condition and progress on a Caring Bridge site. She began ending a daily post with "Ken's scripture for today." Her plan was for me to do my own reports when my health and cognitive abilities enabled me to do so. I wrote my first one on my son's birthday, October 27, 2013. I was finally able to write with some consistency about a month before leaving the hospital.

Soon I began making some observations or reflections on a Bible verse. Over the course of time this has evolved into some daily devotional thoughts that come from my personal Bible reading. At this point we have posted a report or devotional each day for more than two years. This has been an unexpected opportunity to share my journey and some encouragement to others along the way. My experience has deepened my relationship with the Lord and has provided an opportunity to share in a new dimension of "ministry" to others I never anticipated.

These are some of the challenges and experiences I have faced and the changes that have come into my life. I'm glad those have been for my good. What I learned from facing my health crisis is that it not only revealed what I was "made of," but also those around me. I have been challenged and changed and refined. I'm glad with the Lord's help, I have passed the test.

*********************** ***********************

## BETTER OR BITTER?

**BIBLE VERSE FOR TODAY:** *"Here is a trustworthy saying: If we died with him, we will also live with him; if we endure, we will also reign with him. If we disown him, he will also disown us; if we are faithless, he remains faithful, for he cannot disown himself."* —2 Timothy 2:11-13 (NIV)

I have found a life-threatening illness provides an opportunity to reset your priorities. I mentioned to Debbie this morning I recall waking up after my surgery in September 2013 and feeling pretty good physically, but had this sense things were back to "normal" (almost like waking up from a dream). That feeling was somewhat disconcerting. What I desired was to seize the opportunity to reprioritize and to not "waste the suffering."

The old adage is "the troubles of life can make you better or bitter." Many find the trials and sufferings of life lead to questions of why, which can spiral into self-pity, resentment and feeling abandon by God. I remember during therapy, a staff member shared when her father died, she was mad at God. Although it had been years, her faith and confidence in God was still shaken.

Asking "why?" is natural and is not bad. The question of *"Why?"* needs to be followed with *"What now?"* Since I was heavily sedated in those first few weeks, I don't remember having a lot of time to reflect, question and struggle with doubt or resentments. I do recall being mindful of my failings and my misplaced confidence in the things in life that promise a sense of security.

I believe a prayer offered in those early times was the key. I recall my friend Denes Szabo visiting me in the acute care hospital. As I lay in my hospital bed, I asked him if he could scratch the top of my head. I had an annoying itch and was not able to lift my arms due to the paralysis. I recall Denes telling me that he constantly prayed not only for my physical recovery, but that my spiritual and emotional outlook would remain strong. I found the Lord was faithful to answer those prayers in a multitude of ways.

## Chapter 7

# We're in This Together

The foundation of life is found in relationships. We impact others and others impact us. I have found this especially applies to family. Mary Bondi, for a number of years, served as the founding Director of New Hope for Girls. This is a program of Teen Challenge of the Rocky Mountains located in Tooele, Utah. She was known to say, "When one family member is sick [or struggling or fighting an addiction], the whole family is sick."

The bottom line is those closest to us are affected by what happens to us. For example, it is self-evident that for every person fighting an addiction, others are directly impacted. This may be a spouse, child, parent or other family members; as well as employers, co-workers and close friends. Our lives are not lived in isolation. This becomes evident when a health or personal crisis hits.

In my situation, my wife was put into the position of putting her career and life "on hold" while she devoted her time to my care and managing all the details of our home and personal life. My daughter is a young mom living in Atlanta, Georgia. Her youngest, our granddaughter, was seven months old when I was hospitalized.

She dropped her work and family responsibilities to come and help her mom and me. My son-in-law Nathan came and spent as much time as possible and his family helped take up the slack caring for their other two boys when they were away.

My son Christian and his wife Bridget, while living in the Denver area, still made major adjustments in their lives. They had three young children whom Bridget homeschooled and Christian had multiple work responsibilities that often included out-of-state travel.

When I was hospitalized, I was in the process of devoting more time to my work as the Executive Director of Teen Challenge of the Rocky Mountains. We had just finished a quarterly board meeting on Friday, July 19, 2013. I was in the hospital the following Monday, on July 22. This brought about some major adjustments and an improvised "succession" plan to not only handle-day-to day operations, but to deal with some major decisions facing the organization.

Within a matter of days, my family and organization I led found themselves making major adjustments. The health crisis situation for me created a personal crisis situation for many others. This is often the most overlooked and underappreciated aspect of a health crisis. So often, the focus is on the person who is sick, and that is good, but others are impacted as well. I am thankful for the many friends who understood this and prayed for Debbie and my children as well as for me. I am thankful for many who helped with food, cleaned the house, took care of the yard and landscaping, cared for the grandchildren, provided transportation to the airport and helped in many other ways.

Debbie's sister Sue and brother-in-law Sam Schmidt live close to us in Wellington, Colorado. They have been such a great source of help and encouragement in so many ways, including, along with daughter-in-law Bridget, helping manage our family finances.

Debbie made the comment to her sister, "I'm glad this happened when you were so close by." I was touched by her response when she replied, "We would not have done anything different if you were still in Denver; it just made it more convenient." I'm thankful that when it is time for "all hands on deck," there are those who rally to your side and do what needs to be done to get you through the crisis.

In addition to a constant vigil by my bedside and monitoring my condition, my family found themselves taking on whatever tasks and roles were needed. Debbie, with some help from our children, maintained a daily online report of my condition, progress and specific prayer needs. My daughter Stephanie found herself as the "family spokesperson" during a TV news interview. My son Christian found himself giving a speech to a group of legislators, lobbyists and friends gathered near the State Capitol for a fundraiser to cover some of my medical expenses.

As friends and family came to visit, Debbie, Christian and Stephanie became protective of my level of energy and need for rest. They knew I would try to be as hospitable as possible, even in a weakened condition and not able to respond. Stephanie made a sign to help visitors to know what to expect and how to respond. The handwritten sign read:

Rules for Entering Ken's Room

1 – Smile – Don't Cry

2- Speak Positive, Encourage

(He understands what you say)

Our God is a GOOD God!

I am most blessed because of the love of a family that knew how to "rise to the occasion" and to do and get done what needed to be done. This was a time of trust, letting go and understanding what mattered the most.

My health crisis was not only a challenge and life-changing experience for me; it was that for my entire family. My eighty-eight-year-old mother came to visit as often as she could; my sister and brother-in-law Nathalee and Paul Porter came to visit from Highlands Ranch and my older brother Don came from Monterey, California to check on me and encourage me. Even my grandchildren were aware of the challenges I faced and my condition.

It is also during these times that you find out what your life means to your family and to others. While I was hospitalized, son-in-law Nathan considered a job opportunity at our church in Fort Collins. Stephanie and Nathan were still interested in what I thought and sought out my advice. I'm not sure what kind of advice I could give with a swollen brain, but that stimulus could have helped my recovery.

The impact of my crisis on my family and the challenges I faced are reflected in many of their Caring Bridge blog posts. The following, I believe, are especially insightful.

\*\*\*\*\*\*\*\*\*\*\*\*\*\*\*\*\*\*\*\*\*\*\*\*\*\*\*\*

## Stuck in Bed
Christian Summers — August 11, 2013

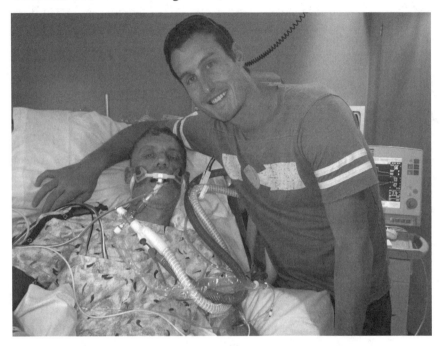

During this health crisis for Dad, it can be easy to talk about the "major" stuff going on, and not all of the residual frustrating issues that can take a toll over weeks of time in bed.

Perhaps you may already know, but it can be easily forgotten how weak dad is, and the reality that he is unable to do anything for himself. He is in essence experiencing paralysis throughout his body. It would be equivalent to ninety percent in lower body, and eight-five percent upper body that lack the ability to move.

Every two hours, the nurses will turn him in bed so he doesn't aggravate the bedsore he has, or incur additional injuries. They have to adjust how his arms are propped, how his legs lay, the direction his feet point, and how pillows support beneath him. We adjust and support his head and neck with a special pillow, in addition to the normal pillows. The head of the bed is raised and lowered to try to provide comfort and relief to his body as it atrophies from the lack of movement and exercise.

We have been incredibly blessed by the nursing staff here at the hospital. Not only are they knowledgeable in their practice of medicine, they are personable in how they listen and talk with us about the concerns we have for dad, and that he be comfortable and his pain be minimized. We have to try and read his facial expressions and how he motions with his hands to understand what he needs.

We ask a lot of "yes and no" questions to try and determine what he needs in the moment. It would probably be humorous, if it weren't so frustrating. I often feel helpless; I can't imagine how he must feel to be "trapped" in his own body.

He isn't able to swallow well or cough, so we try to help the nursing staff, when we must suction his mouth, so he doesn't choke or aspirate. He always wants ice chips, which is all he's allowed orally due to aspiration risk. I'm not sure I could give him too many, but I do have to make sure he's fully swallowed all of it before giving anymore.

Today, for a few minutes, we were able to "talk" with dad. This is enabled by him being taken off of the ventilator in his "trach" and a passymuer valve put in. This device caps the trach tube. When this is done, he is able to breathe in through the tube in his neck, and then exhale through his mouth, which activates the vocal chords on command. While faint and hard to understand, dad was able to "voice" his response to questions and ask a couple of his own. I'm pretty sure he asked for coffee.

Dad has not lost his fighting spirit through all of this. We talked about the setbacks he's facing and the new treatment plan of action, and the decisions we are making for him, and if he agreed with us and trusted what we were doing. He replied, "Absolutely."

Please pray for us as we strive to care for dad alongside the health care professionals. It's so draining and hard to see my strong dad, so weakened and incapacitated. For now we are keeping our eyes on Jesus as our healer and hope. We are confident that He will give us the strength that we need and sustain us regardless of what the future holds.

## A Hard Mile

Christian Summers — August 13, 2013

Today dad is tired. He has stayed asleep pretty much all day. Yesterday he had a big day with a lot of activity, including his treatment. If I'm being honest, he admitted he's a little discouraged today. I can only imagine what he must feel like emotionally, much less physically. I asked him if he feels like giving up, he shook his head, "No."

We've come to make running analogies, as a way to relate how he's feeling. I asked him if this is a hard mile today; he shook his head, "Yes." If you know anything about running, you know that there are days when a run doesn't go well or where things don't "click." Today is one of those days.

If you know my dad, you know that a hard mile won't stop him or keep him discouraged, because tomorrow is a new day, and the next step brings a new mile. Perhaps the next mile brings breakthrough's we've been praying for, perhaps dad finds his rhythm and stride, where he can see the finish line ahead.

Ultimately, we know we all have a finish line we will cross. When the steps we take each day will cease. When we will stand before He who created us, and answer for the race we ran.

In that moment, dad will be able to answer like Paul, when he wrote Timothy: *"I have fought the good fight, I have finished the race, I have kept the faith"* (1 Timothy 4:7, NIV).

Perhaps, dad still has a lot of time before that day, perhaps not; but the reality is, none of us know what tomorrow will bring. Don't allow a "hard mile" to derail that which God is doing in you and through you. Stay faithful!

Take a moment to quietly reflect. Ask yourself, "Have I been faithful? Is each moment of my life pointing toward Jesus and giving Him glory? Do I live my days in my own strength and wisdom, or in His? Do I love others like Jesus does?"

Dad's verse today (may it be yours as well): *"I consider my life worth nothing to me; my only aim is to finish the race and complete the task the Lord Jesus has given me—the task of testifying to the good news of God's grace"* (Acts 20:24, NIV).

## A New Reality

Stephanie Munn, August 25, 2013

Our family has a "new" reality. It has been over a month now since my phone has rung and I have seen "Dad" appear on the call ID. This is my "new" reality.

Since my dad has been hospitalized, I have been there sixteen out of the thirty-five days. As I return to my life in Georgia, I can't help but feel an emotion of guilt as I have to pick up the pieces of my life while supporting my mother and father who are going through this tragedy.

Without a doubt, this guilt does not come from my father nor my mother as they want our lives to continue; but it still simply feels weird. It feels different enjoying a day at the pool, taking family pictures and planning a future vacation.

Then it hits me... I don't know the date or time when my dad will walk through the front door of my home and step into my life, like he has so often.

I have no idea of how much he will miss out on during this journey and that makes me sad. He has six active grandchildren who have a fallen hero. We have tried our best to keep them innocent to the tragedy but they all know their grandpa is missing.

No one has been more affected than my mom. She has temporarily left her full-time job, to sit at the hospital everyday for twelve plus hours to help make medical decisions and support my father. She has been a pillar of strength, yet I know in the quietness of the night she still has missed the "normalcy" of yesterday.

As for Christian, I know he has lost his best friend. Since I live out of state, my parents have been more actively involved with Christian, his wife Bridget, and children Riley, Cade and Eliana.

For me, Nathan, my husband, Mason, Carter and Mckenzie, we will return to Colorado as much as possible as we walk through this experience. I used to talk with my mom every other day but now I can't help but call her every other hour.

While my dad continues to love us all and support us in this "new" reality, I still have hope that he will return to the "normalcy" we have known him to possess.

In the meantime, we still continue to strive and succeed in all that he has raised us to be. We will honor him by taking care of his six precious jewels (grandchildren) and create a life for them of happiness and joy.

Verse for the day: *"I waited patiently for the Lord, and He inclined to me, and He heard my cry. He also brought me up out of a horrible pit. Out of the miry clay, and set my feel upon a rock, and established my steps"* (Psalm 40:1-2, NIV).

**Turning Nightmares into Dreams**
Stephanie Munn, November 10, 2013

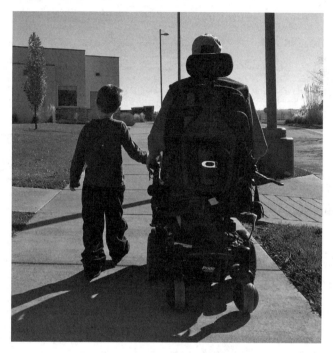

Those who know me well know that I refer to the last few months as "our nightmare." I honestly don't think that my dad could have endured much more.

As children, we all learn from our parents. Christian and I, along with our spouses, have found my mom and dad so faithful in our intimate circle of this season.

My mom's faith has never wavered. She continues to show me how to be a faithful wife through the darkest days. I adore her overwhelming positive spirit and how she watches with grace every word that comes out of her mouth. She is patient. She is intentional to make sure that they don't make life all about them. She finds ways to bless others and make them feel valuable as they care for my dad.

My dad has lost a lot of the identity and dignity that he had known. Yet, his fight along with his faith, remain strong, while everything else is weak.

As children, we have found our parents faithful to everything they would have hoped that they would be, if anything like this was to ever happen. Then, we also notice a generation behind us. These six grandchildren are forever changed by this experience. For their entire life, they will see a wheelchair as an invitation, not a barrier. They will see someone who is sick as a testimony, not a disease.

And then I realize, this nightmare just might lead us to our dreams!

****************************

I am not only pleased that I have survived a health crisis, but I am gratified by the great extent to which my family stood by my side, faced the challenges with me and passed the test. I can relate to the Apostle John's words, *"I have no greater joy than to hear that my children are walking in the truth"* (3 John 4, ESV). But just as the Lord was faithful to me through my family, support came from many others and from some unexpected sources.

## Chapter 8

# Encouragement from Unexpected Sources

*"A friend loves at all times, and a brother is born for adversity."* (Proverbs 17:7 ESV)

I f you want to find out your flaws and discover your enemies, face unjust criticism and deal with "fair weather" friends, run for political office. If you want to experience true support and encouragement and discover those who value you, then see who surfaces when you face a crisis. As it became evident that my hospitalization had turned into a more serious illness than could be anticipated, the calls, cards and expressions of concern and support came rushing in.

The response my family received demonstrated how much people were concerned and wanted to help; it also created a challenge on how to respond and manage visitors. Debbie did an excellent job with Christian and Stephanie's help. As I mentioned, she, believing we were in for more of an extended illness, set up a Caring Bridge site to report regular updates on my condition. This helped people monitor my progress and keep informed on my needs.

There were calls and visits from a host of friends and other family members who called to express their concern and offer to help in "any way they could." This included friends from the "State House" to the "Church House."

Southern Gales Church was located in my House District while I served in the Colorado House. Besides being acquainted with the church from my pastoral connection as a neighboring congregation, individuals in this church took an active role in practicing "biblical citizenship." As a result some key individuals from the church were instrumental in supporting my political service.

The Day by Day Sunday School Class at Southern Gales Church became a steady source of help and encouragement. They sent cards, prayed and provided financial support. As a result, one of my first trips to Denver as I recovered was to this dedicated group of supporters.

One of the more interesting stories involves three brothers who are all fellow Assemblies of God ministers. Michael Popineau, the Senior Pastor of First Assembly in Greeley; his brother Loren, the Senior Pastor of Family Worship Center in Centennial, Colorado was also on the Teen Challenge Board; and brother Randy who lives in Colorado Springs and serves as one of the Executive Officers for the Assemblies of God in Colorado and Utah.

The Popineau brothers grew up in the home of a dedicated church layman who was also a professional painter. Randy and his wife Joan came to visit me when I was in the Long Term Acute Care Hospital. During the visit, Randy asked, "Is there anything we can do?" Debbie said, "Well, Ken was in the process of painting our bathrooms when he was hospitalized and they have never been finished." I was a little embarrassed by her request of three busy ministry leaders and communicated that was too much to ask.

I thought that had ended the issue and over the next several weeks I had forgotten the visit and conversation. One day, when Debbie and I ate dinner in the rehabilitation hospital, she reminded me of Randy and Joan's visit many weeks earlier. She mentioned Michael, Loren and Randy had painted our bathrooms. My response was, "I thought I told you they were too busy!" She said, "I know, but I overruled you!" I will always remember this generous act of support and the kindness of my three friends.

The end of my first week in the hospital was the annual Western Conservative Summit in Denver. This event hosted by Colorado Christian University and the Centennial Institute was quickly becoming a weekend political affairs conference with a national reputation. Debbie and I had planned to attend the conference and she said she remembered me stating I thought I would be out of the hospital in time for us to attend!

The news of my hospitalization quickly spread during the conference. John Andrews, former State Senate President and founder of the Centennial Institute gave a report about my condition and requested prayer for my family and me. One year later, when I was able to once again attend this conference, John shared his reflections by commenting, "By the questions I was asked by reporters, it sounded like they had prepared for a eulogy." I was glad I survived and was able attend, even if it was in a wheelchair.

When I went into a crisis and Debbie walked away from her job, we were not certain when she would return and what kind of expenses we would incur even if we were able to maintain health insurance. We quickly found regardless of how financially secure you believe you are, a health crisis can undermine that confidence in a short time. We are grateful and indebted for the support of Halcyon

Hospice, who continued our health insurance and held Debbie's job until she could return to work.

My adult children's employers were also an important source of support. Stephanie has worked for over ten years for Access Property Management in Atlanta. Her employer has been tremendously supportive of her as a young mother in her work as their Marketing Manager. This support was extended in giving her the time to make frequent trips to Colorado. Christian's work with Apartment Life Ministries and Mile High Vineyard also required their support in order for him to come during times of crisis not only during my initial hospitalization, but in the year that followed.

In response to our need, Teen Challenge set up a "medical relief" fund to receive donations to pay for out-of-pocket medical expenses and ongoing therapy. Friends began to respond from all over the country. One of those was Robert and Patricia Polvado from Oklahoma. When Debbie and I were in college, Robert served as the District Youth Director for Assemblies of God Churches in Colorado and Utah. We had not kept in touch over the years, but when he found out about my illness, they responded in the most generous and encouraging manner.

My father's cousin Courtland Rybicka, a wheat farmer from Strasburg, was a confidant to me in my days when I served on the School Board in that community. He then donated to my campaigns during my legislative years. When he learned of my health crisis he not only responded with immediate generosity, but his continued support has enabled me to access the rehabilitation services needed to achieve my goal of full recovery. I know my father (who worked for Courtland's father when he was first married) would be pleased with this outpouring of support and generosity. Last year I was honored to attend Courtland's 90th birthday celebration.

The current Speaker of the Colorado House, Democrat Mark Ferindino and the former Speaker of the House, Republican Frank McNulty, went together to co-host a fundraiser held near the Capitol in Denver. The event was attended by a host of legislators, lobbyists and friends. One of the biggest promoters of the event was State Senator Andy Kerr who had defeated me in the 2012 election. Some of the Denver news channels also reported about the event and our need.

When I finally returned home and became aware of all that transpired and saw the number and list of names of those who had donated, it was humbling. The list included almost as many individuals that I did not know along with those I did know. There were those I would not have expected to hear from as much as those that I did. This once again demonstrated how individuals are willing to respond to a need and demonstrate their support in a time of crisis. This motivates an individual to keep working and not give up.

The legislative colleague that has provided ongoing support and encouragement is Spencer Swalm from Centennial. Spencer and I were both elected in 2006 and had been part of a political discussion group known as the Vanguard Forum. This group produced at least four state legislators and others who served in elected office on the city and county level. In the time since returning home Spencer has made several trips to Fort Collins to encourage me and take Debbie and me out to lunch.

House Sergeant Leon Brandli usually accompanies him. I actually met Leon when I served as a pastor. He was always a man dedicated to prayer. When I was in the State House, I discovered Leon was employed by the Department of Revenue that was located next to the Capitol. He would spend his lunchtime in prayer, often going to the top of the dome where he had a view of the entire city. When he retired from the Department of Revenue, he became a House Sergeant and became acquainted with several legislators, including Spencer.

My friend David Warren has been an unexpected source of support. Dave has one the most interesting political histories as an active citizen of anyone I know, dating back to the Barry Goldwater days. I met David through a Republican breakfast club, but since he wasn't in my House District, he was cordial, but had not been that supportive during my campaigns. However, in the 2012 election for the State Senate, he got behind me in donating to my campaign and walking door to door with me on several occasions. After I returned home from the hospital, David visited me several times when he and his wife visited family in Fort Collins. This was a friendship that developed toward the end of my political career that provided some appreciated personal support as well.

Another unexpected source of encouragement came through the "Get Well" cards I received. During my illness, I receive hundreds of "Get Well" cards, and then I celebrated my sixtieth birthday while in the rehabilitation hospital. Debbie and our friend Cyndy Luzinski taped all the cards to the walls of my room. It was a visual reminder that I was "surrounded" by support. It was amazing that with so many cards, few were the same.

Some of those cards were handmade cards from my sister-in-law's fourth grade class. Claudia Summers, my brother's wife in Monterey, teaches at a school with a high number of low-income children. She told them about my illness and had them write me a "Get Well" card as an assignment. I was impressed by the notes inside when I received them. One of them, I will never forget. The message read, "We are all counting on you to get better!" Whenever I needed encouragement, I reminded myself of that card from an unknown fourth grader in Monterey, California.

After being a pastor for almost twenty-eight years, Debbie and I spent six years as regular church attendees while I served in the legislature. We had just moved to Fort Collins and reconnected with Timberline Church, which was Debbie's family church in Fort Collins, and is pastored by our friend Dary Northrop. We had attended the church about three weeks when I was hospitalized. In spite of our new status, the support we received from "our church" was consistent and comforting.

Pastor Steve Harris and Visitation Pastor John Engle kept in constant touch and made frequent visits. This was in addition to many long time friends and new friends that came along side of us in our time of need.

I have known Steve Harris and his family for over thirty years. This reconnection after many years came at an opportune time. Steve kept in constant contact during my initial and subsequent hospitalizations. When I returned home, Steve would visit me during my homebound recovery, bringing lunch for us to enjoy together. He has continued to be a source of encouragement throughout my recovery. Steve's wife Sherri, several years ago, was diagnosed with MS. This made a special connection and provided me insight as I learned to deal with my own neuromuscular disorder.

Pastor John Engle was well acquainted with Debbie's mother before she passed away and we quickly connected with his concern and attention. Over the course of almost five months, John became like family. On one occasion, he visited after my surgery when a nurse came into the room. She said, "You have a visitor!" I thought she meant someone had just arrived, but then she motioned toward Pastor John. I responded, "Oh, that's just John!"

The Sunday after I was hospitalized, Debbie attended the service at Timberline Church with Christian. At the end of the service they went forward to connect with a prayer team member about my situation. They met Ted and Murlene Grizzle, who they discovered lived not far from our home in Fort Collins. As we got acquainted with Ted and Murlene, we found they had attended a church in Denver that we were familiar with and we knew some of the same people. They became fast friends, visiting me in the hospital, helping with work around the house and providing transportation to appointments when I returned home.

In moving to Fort Collins we looked forward to reconnecting with our long-time friends Ron and Dixie Kee. They have been family friends of ours and Debbie's parents for years, going back to our college days. I was hospitalized before we had an opportunity to renew our friendship, but they were quick to "step up to the plate" and do whatever was needed in many ways, from providing airport transportation for Stephanie to visiting me in the hospital to modifying doors in our home so I could navigate with my wheelchair around the house.

During Debbie's parents' life, they were known to embrace college students attending Colorado State University and other young couples. They served as friends, encouragers and mentors. One of those young couples in Isla's (Debbie's mother) final years was Zane Strange and his wife, Jenny. Zane was a project director for Serve 6.8, a nonprofit established out of Timberline Church to serve the practical needs of the community. It was Serve 6.8 whose volunteers directed by Zane built the handicap ramp that enabled me to have access to our home when I was released from the hospital. I'm sure Debbie's mom would have been proud of one of the young men she befriended.

While the ramp was constructed, Debbie received a call from Steve Grims, who Zane had asked to serve as the project coordinator. As they talked on the phone, Debbie found out that he was dating a woman by the name of Loni. Loni had been a roommate of Debbie's in college and was working as a nurse practitioner in Fort Collins and this event provided the opportunity to reconnect after many years. Steve not only helped with constructing the ramp, but also some steps to help me recover from a fall and then returned over a year later to dismantle the ramp as I arrived at that point in my recovery.

When it came to pastoral support, my friend Bob Strauch was an added and unexpected source of encouragement. I met Bob in college and played competitive fast pitch softball. We both went into teaching in the Englewood Public Schools. I only taught two years before going into ministry. On the other hand, Bob had a long tenure as a middle school teacher and coach. However, in time, he followed the Lord's call on his life into full-time ministry. For twenty years he served the small rural community of Flagler, Colorado.

It had been years since I had seen Bob, but during my legislative years we saw each other occasionally at the Capitol because his son Nate was involved in political work. Bob heard about my illness from our mutual friend Steve Cohen. Steve had been one of my junior high teachers whom I kept in touch with through the years. He was also the principal of the school where Bob taught. Steve had heard the report of my hospitalization on the radio and shared it with Bob during one of their regular times of conversation.

Bob wasn't sure where I was hospitalized, but searched and used some of his son's contacts to find out. He came to see me and was a regular visitor, being present at critical times and always sharing a scripture verse and prayer as part of our time together. He was present the day I came home from the hospital and read scripture and had one final prayer with a large group of family and friends who gathered as I left my hospital room for home.

During my recovery, I needed medical equipment to function outside of the hospital setting. That included a power wheelchair and a vehicle I could ride in.

My father was the oldest of ten children in his family. One of his sisters, Joanne, had polio as a young teen. She met and married Victor Beebe from Loveland who was also a polio victim. They lived in a house Vic had built to accommodate their needs. For years, they were advocates for the disability community in Loveland and northern Colorado.

Joanne actually helped my father name me when I was born. My mother came up with my older brother's name, which was Donald Eugene, because he was born on my parent's anniversary and my father's brother's (Gene) birthday. When they found out they had a second son, my mom looked at my dad and said, "I named the first; you have to name the second." So, my dad consulted his sister and they came up with the name Kenneth Guy. I'm not sure about the name Kenneth, but Guy is my paternal grandfather's name.

As Debbie and I anticipated moving to Fort Collins at some future date, I thought it would be providential that we would be only six miles from my aunt and uncle's home. However, by the time we moved, my aunt had passed away from a long-standing battle with cancer. When I was first hospitalized, my Uncle Vic was down the hall from my room fighting his own failing health. Just a month later, Vic also passed away.

While the loss of my aunt and uncle destroyed my plans for the future, it provided an unexpected blessing. In their later years, they needed power wheelchairs for their mobility and also had a handicap van. My Aunt Paula Baer, my father's youngest sibling, had provided care to her sister and brother-in-law and served as their personal representative.

Paula switched her care giving that she had provided her sister and brother-in-law to her nephew who now faced a health crisis. She kept in constant touch and made me a quilt that adorned my hospital bed and continues to be a treasured possession. She made it possible for me to not only have the use of my Uncle Vic's power wheelchair, but also their handicap van. This was a blessing and provision that is hard to imagine being without. I'm sure my father, who passed away many years before, would have been proud of the care his "baby sister" provided his son.

As I waited for my surgery as a patient in the long term acute care hospital, it appeared there were issues that arose with my care or other complications that kept prolonging my surgery schedule. I told Debbie we needed a "no more crises" approach for the days leading up to surgery.

Nighttime was especially challenging. I was not only concerned about the attention from the staff, but I was still on a respirator. Because of my paralysis and the inflated support cushion on my bed, I could not reach the bed controls to adjust the bed. Debbie put out a call and several individuals stepped forward to volunteer to spend the night with me. This dedicated group included Pastor Bob Strauch, Pastor Jim Brummett, Helen Parton (a nursing colleague of Debbie's), Shirley Seitz (who had supported me in my political career), Gwen Kovac (who was a retired missionary and friend from our college days), Ron Graham (who had attended our church in Littleton), Sue Mastin and Lucie Baca (who were friends of Gwen's who I had never met but volunteered to help) and my long time friend Rod Carlson, who was in town during their itinerary with their Living Logos scripture presentation ministry.

Throughout most of the time as a patient in the rehabilitation hospital, our long time family friend David Holden would come and have dinner with me and spend a few hours every Saturday evening until I was ready to go to sleep. This provided Debbie a break and allowed her to attend a Saturday evening church service.

David's father and Debbie's mother graduated from high school together. Later on, both of their parents attended Bible College together to train for ministry. The two families had remained friends throughout the years. David's father was the denominational representative I was under when I served in my first pastorate. So, this ended up being a connection with some great family history.

One of the first hospital visitors was high school classmate Debbie Proctor. Debbie lived in Loveland and had just retired from her career as a high school teacher. I'm not sure how she found out about my hospitalization so quickly and I didn't recall her living in Loveland. She became a great source of help in tending to the many rose bushes around the house and keeping some of my former classmates from high school informed about my condition.

Debbie was assisted in some of the outside care of our home by Bill Hutchinson. Bill and his wife had rented our home the year before we moved to Fort Collins. Even though he worked in Cheyenne, he still took time to stop by the house to help whenever he could.

Help with keeping up the house came from our friend Kathleen Talkington. Kathleen and her husband Dave and family attended our church in Strasburg, Colorado. They had moved to Texas for several years, but had recently moved back to Colorado and settled in Greeley, close to Fort Collins.

There were many other "old" friends and "new" who did so much and were willing to help whenever and wherever they could; so many did so much to help "cover the bases." This proved to us how faithful the Lord is to provide in ways that we would never have imagined. Many of those who helped have their own "God stories" of how it worked out for them to be available to assist.

What is important when the difficulties of life come and trials assail and our faith is tested is to the see God's hand working in the situations we face. We often become so focused on what is happening to us and asking why, we get stuck in self-pity and reflection and miss out on what is happening around us. We need to "spy God" working in dramatic and subtle ways He chooses to bring us help, encouragement and healing. If we do that, we will find the encouragement that keeps us pushing to each new day. We will also be surprised how He works through others and in unexpected ways.

## Chapter 9

# Care Givers: Making a Difference in Those Who Make a Difference in You

"**C**ode Ken in ten minutes." It was December 10, 2013. The announcement over the hospital PA system informed staff that I would soon be leaving for home. In a hospital a "code blue" signals someone in distress, but Northern Colorado Rehabilitation Hospital made it a practice to use a special "code" to signal good news, a patient is graduating from therapy and returning home. The staff members would line the hallway leading to the main entrance and applaud as the patient was wheeled out to the vehicle waiting to take them home.

It had been sixty days since I had been admitted to inpatient rehabilitation. The normal stay is about two weeks, sometimes up to four. Because of my condition, I was afforded an extended amount of time. I was glad to have the time, because when I thought I would be returning home in the previous month, my anxiety level was high. One of the nurses felt I was becoming "institutionalized," a condition where you adjust so much to your hospital setting, it feels normal. However, I realized on November 10 that I still had some significant medical needs that would require special attention. Even though I was not able to return home for my birthday, the ensuing four weeks allowed many issues to be addressed. Finally, I was ready for my homecoming, just in time for Christmas.

There were ten family members, friends and pastors in my hospital room waiting for the final papers to be signed for my release. We enjoyed a time of reflection, scripture reading and prayer. Finally all the papers were signed and it was time for me to navigate my power wheelchair down the hall and out the front doors of the hospital.

As I made my way toward the front entrance with Debbie by my side and family and friends in tow, the line of staff members that formed the aisle for me to traverse seemed to extend from the hospital lobby to the doorway that leads to patient rooms. One of my friends said he counted about 100 people. There were staff members from both hospital units where I had been a patient. Represented in the group were medical and patient care staff, therapists, administrators, maintenance personnel, cooks and members of the housekeeping team. It was a humbling and emotional send off. I stopped and turned my wheelchair toward the group and shared my thanks and encouraged them in their work.

My lengthy hospitalization and trips between McKee Hospital and Northern Colorado Rehabilitation Hospital made me known to many of the doctors and staff members, even those who weren't involved in my care. When a doctor would come in to see me and do a check up or evaluation, Debbie would have them write their name on the white board in my room. At one time the list included thirteen doctors who had been to see me.

While I was in a condition where I was unaware of my surroundings and who was in the room, Debbie established relationships with all of the staff regardless of who they were. She could pull up their names, where they lived, how long they had worked at the hospital and something about their personal life. Maybe that is a stretch for all of them, but it was true for many. Debbie's background as a nurse certainly created a unique point of understanding and identification. The concern Debbie showed for those who cared for me made for some significant connections. Having never been in a hospital, I realize now how important it is to care for those who care for you.

After I left the hospital, I would return for outpatient therapy or for other reasons. When staff members greeted me they would immediately ask how Debbie was doing. I got use to the greeting, "Ken, good to see you, how's Debbie?"

One of the few members of the medical staff at McKee Hospital who I remember is Gary Harkness. Gary was my physical therapist and had a son attending Faith Christian High School in Arvada. I was friends with a teacher he knew from the school. Besides being a knowledgeable and competent therapist, Gary was a man of faith. As a result, he not only was of great value to my physical needs, but also a source of spiritual encouragement.

At one time when I faced a difficult time, Debbie talked to Gary and he shared a perspective that became one of our themes during my hospitalization. Gary simply told Debbie, "Stay the course. Keep your eyes on the cross." After leaving McKee Hospital near the end of August, I would return about a month later for surgery. I would reconnect with Gary during that time. We would continue to stay in touch and Gary would come to visit me in the rehabilitation hospital and even visited me with his son Grant at our home in Fort Collins.

I found, like in any relationship or environment, there are those with whom, by virtue of their personality, knowledge or commitment to their work, you developed more of a connection. That created greater comfort when they were assigned to your care and at times more anxiety when it was someone else. That certainly was the case during the night more than the day. I'm thankful for those who were patient when I would ask for a certain nurse or therapist to perform a procedure or care provider to transfer me until I was able to build that confidence with a greater number of people.

As the Chair of the Health Committee at the State House, and having a wife as a nurse, I felt I was fairly familiar with the health care environment. When it comes to health care, the topics focus on access to care, affordability of care and quality of care.

Our public policy discussions usually focused on the first two. I felt the quality piece wasn't as significant in light of access to care and the affordability of care. Of course, I had never been a patient and my medical care consisted of an occasional visit to a primary care physician every two or three years. When I became a "real" patient and one for an extended period of time, I was able to see some of the challenges that still exist with quality of care. I tell people, "When the care is good, there is nothing like it; and when the care is bad, there is nothing like it."

I am pleased when I look back on my 140-plus days of hospitalization in 2013 and thirty or more in 2014, I have few complaints. The issues that did arise we were able to address. Of course it does feel a little strange when you return to the hospital and you call in your meal request and the voice on the phone says, "Welcome back!" As my primary care physician called the hospital for one of my readmits, they asked for my name. When they were told my name, the admission personnel at the hospital responded, "Oh, we know who he is!"

There are so many who cared for me either for an extended or short period of time. It is difficult to identify them by name and their impact on my life. It was interesting to find many of those taking care of me were people of faith, several who attended our e church. I am certainly thankful for Rachel, my physical therapist for sixty days who literally got me "back on my feet" at least to some extent. I found out that Rachel attends my church and also was familiar with the work of Teen Challenge. My occupational therapists were both named "Katie," who I affectionately referred to as "Katie-one" and "Katie-two."

One day my hospital room door was open when I heard a therapist walking a patient in the hallway comment as they came to my door, "This is the happiest room in the hospital." As my time in the hospital extended closer to the end of the year, Debbie decided to brighten my room with a small Christmas tree. This added to the décor with all of the get well cards and birthday cards that lined the walls. As a result, it became a room that staff members didn't mind coming to.

During the night, I would often have some background noise on my phone that sounded like rain or a calming stream of water. One night a nurse came into check on me and she lingered for a while by my bedside. She was having a stressful night. She said, "It is so peaceful in this room, I just need to pause for a few moments before I continue my rounds."

My determination to improve and the support of Debbie, my family and so many friends was not lost on the medical staff. Several people made comments about the support structure I had over the course of my hospitalization. One respiratory therapist who became a good friend expressed with some anxiety to me that if he were in my situation, he didn't know if he would have anywhere close to the same amount of support.

I tell people that we can have faith and be confident of victory over the challenges we face, but we all need help to stay focused and encouraged. In the gospels is found the miracle of the healing of a paralyzed man. This man was carried by four friends and was lowered through the roof of the house to Jesus. Scripture records that Jesus paid special attention to the faith of his friends who carried him to Jesus. It is the only time in the Bible when Jesus commends faith that it is possessed by someone other than the person in need. (Matthew 9:1-8). I am thankful for the "faith for others" that makes a difference and stands as a testament to the Lord's faithfulness.

Being in the hospital, I knew my recovery depended upon those who provided for my care. The quality of my recovery would be directly related to the quality of the staff and the care I received. I didn't anticipate how I responded as a patient and especially the interaction that Debbie had with others and the example of her life would make such a lasting impact on those who cared for me.

## Chapter 10

# An Eye on the Rearview Mirror

As you drive toward a new destination, you glance at your rearview mirror. Besides being a safety issue, you are reminded about where you were and where you are headed. If you focus too much on where you have been, it will create danger in moving forward. Such is the case in the journey of our life.

"Don't waste your suffering." It has been so long since I heard or read that statement that I can't remember where it was from. However, I've come to understand the truth behind it. To go through a life-threatening illness and a prolonged recovery without a greater appreciation for life and being changed by the experience to me does feel like a "waste." I'm not sure if I am always able to appreciate or successfully articulate all of my "lessons learned." I still find myself in times of reflection or reading something and making a connection to what is communicated about life and challenges that come our way. In addition to what I have shared, here are a few that have "stuck with me."

**Never Say "Never"**

*"What could possibly go wrong?"* Those were my exact words to Debbie on a number of occasions. Often during a conversation about our finances—what we had and where the information was and how to access it, Debbie would invariably make the statement, "I hope nothing happens to you; I'm not sure what I would do!" I would endeavor to relieve her anxiety by pointing to the program on the computer showing the location of files and other information. I would conclude by saying, "What could possibly go wrong? I'm healthy and active and have never had any serious health issues!"

Much to my surprise, I found out how quickly life can change. I was familiar with scriptures that warn us about the brevity and uncertainties of life. Scriptures like: *"Do not boast about tomorrow, for you do not know what a day may bring"* (Proverbs 27:1, ESV). *"Teach us to realize the brevity of life, so that we may grow in wisdom"* (Psalm 90:12, NLT). *"Lord, remind me how brief my time on earth will be. Remind me that my days are numbered—how fleeting my life is"* (Psalm 39:4, NLT). *"You do not even know what will happen tomorrow. What is your life? You are a mist that appears for a little while and then vanishes"* (James 4:14, NIV).

As a pastor, there were many occasions when I was shocked by the sudden death of a church member. There were those times that an individual was alive and well and in church on Sunday, and I stood at their casket doing their funeral by Friday. What I found was:

**1 – We can understand the brevity of life for others, but not for ourselves.**

It is easy to have a cognitive sense of what the Bible says, because we can see it in the daily news and we experience with those we know in our own life. When my son was a child, his response to me when I corrected him was often, "I know, I know!!" Usually to which I would respond, "No, you don't know, because you would behave differently!" I felt like the Lord tried to show me through my crisis how fragile life is and to not take it for granted. It was like I said through my actions and attitude, "I know, I know!" Then it was like God said, "You don't know," but I do now!

**2 – We don't value what we have in life until life changes.**

It is easy to take life for granted, to believe what is will always be and what I have will never change. Consider Job's perspective of his life: *"I thought, 'I will live for as many days as there are grains of sand, and I will die in my own house...The dew will lie on the branches all night. New honors will come to me continually, and I will always have great strength'"* (Job 29:18-20, NCV).

Life changed quickly for Job and life, as I knew it, changed quickly for me. When that happens, we realize where we have placed our attention, time and efforts has been misplaced. In a moment of time all that has formed a sense of security and confidence in life can be gone or radically changed. At the same time, there is an opportunity to appreciate and value what matters most: our relationship with God and our family and friends and health.

**3 — The life we live, the decisions we make and where we place our trust and faith today determines our destiny for eternity.**

I am thankful that I have had the opportunity, as a pastor, to help people "get their house in order" before they died; but not everyone has that opportunity. Every day, we need to ask ourselves, "Am I prepared for eternity if this is my last day on earth?" That not only means my relationship with the Lord, but my relationship with others. It means asking ourselves the question, "Have I made the practical decisions and preparations so my spouse and family will not be unduly handicapped as they face the future?"

### 4 — "Success" in life is not the same as the "Impact" of your life.

We all desire to have a "successful life." We want our children to have a life of "success." I am thankful we can trust the Lord to bless the "work of our hands" and "crown us with favor and success." However, if we focus the value of our life on professional or business "success" or achievement, we may be disappointed. If we compare ourselves to others, we will find there are those who do "better" than we do and those who do "worse."

I am pleased I have had some "successful endeavors," but I'm not sure if I looked at my life by many criteria, I would say I was a "success." My years as a pastor didn't result in the numeric growth and impact on a community I would have anticipated. My years as a legislator compared to others did not reflect many "life changing" or "cutting edge" polices.

What I have found is "success in life" as many would measure it, does not always equate to the "impact of your life." During my health crisis, I was surprised, pleased and humbled by the number and variety of individuals that I have known throughout my life, who expressed their appreciation for what I had meant to them and how I had influenced them. It may have been subtle for some, more direct for others. What I learned is people are looking. They are paying attention to your life and the impact of your life is not measured in the same way as we often view "success" in life.

**5 — Prayer makes a difference.**

I believe in prayer and the power of prayer. Like many, my consistency and faithfulness in prayer as a spiritual discipline could use some improvement; yet my life and progress is a testimony to answered prayer. I believe that! So often we view answers to prayer in terms of the grand and the miraculous and miss the answers to prayer that come in our day-to-day lives.

During my hospitalization and recovery, it was heartwarming to hear of those who prayed for me across the country and literally around the world. During my surgery in September of 2013, a group of Filipino pastors prayed fervently for me. I had been to the Philippines on several occasions to participate as a speaker at a pastors' conference and many of these had become dear friends. Even though it had been years since my last trip, they still remembered me and honored me with their prayers.

I recall seeing Missionary Jim Mazurek, a friend of mine from Chile, at a pastor's gathering in Denver in 2015. He was pleased to see me and told me that people prayed for me in South America. I know there were several churches in Colorado aware of my health crisis and prayed for me. This included churches and individuals from around the country. I continually hear of reports about churches who have prayed for me. Recently, a cousin at a family gathering said she still has people from her church asking her, "How is Ken?" It was always encouraging to hear of those who had prayed for me; even from some people that I didn't realize believed in prayer!

As Debbie gave daily reports on my physical condition through Caring Bridge, she soon began listing specific prayer requests. Our friend Cyndy Luzinski had just finished reading Pastor Mark Batterson's book, *Prayer Circles,* and told Debbie how she read the

"Lord is not offended by bold requests. He is offended by anything less." As a result, Debbie began reporting and compiling specific prayer needs for each day.

I was always pleased when I heard individuals share how they had made a commitment to pray for Debbie as well as me. That is certainly an important need to remember when someone is in a health crisis. It is important for people to pray for a spouse and family members as they provide support to their loved one and deal with all the challenges that come during those times.

Although individuals when they visited would pray for me before they left, one of the most vivid "answers to prayer" came when no one was noticeably praying. I was at McKee Hospital recovering from my surgery, and the respiratory therapist was talking about the decision to remove my trach hardware or to insert a smaller device. We weighed the pros and cons and she planned on completely removing the hardware in my throat when she was delayed because of the needs of other patients. During that time we re-evaluated the options. Debbie was in my room with my brother and sister-in-law, along with my friend Bob Strauch. When the respiratory therapist came in, she told us since it was late in the day, so she would wait for tomorrow to remove the trach hardware.

As we considered this decision with a high degree of anxiety, it was like a "wave of peace" entered the room and we all together looked at each and said, "Let's have them size down the hardware, not remove it." What is interesting, I wasn't sure if anyone else had any sense of "divine intervention" until my brother-in-law commented about it to me later. He said, "I felt something as we made that decision, I thought Bob was probably praying." He may have been;

I never asked, but I know the Lord intervened with some wisdom in that moment that was borne out in the coming weeks.

### Trusting God – Trusting Others

Just like not grasping the fragileness of life until life is threatened, the same can be true when it comes to trusting the Lord. It is one thing to say, "I am trusting in the Lord" when it appears we control our destiny; it is another thing to "trust in the Lord" when life is uncertain and doctors are as confused about your condition and future.

Job said, *"My ears had heard of you before, but now my eyes have seen you"* (Job 42:5, NCV). To go through a health crisis or a life crisis and not gain a different understanding and perspective of the Lord feels like a lost opportunity. There are times in my life when uncertainties did require a complete trust in the Lord, but none like those that arise when your life and your future is on the line. The questions surrounding my condition during my health crisis ranged from "will he survive?" to "what level of cognitive ability will he have?" to "will he have a permanent disability?"

I can relate to the prayer of David when he said, *"LORD, I put my life in your hands. I trust in you, my God, and I will not be disappointed"* (Psalm 25:1-2, ESV). Even as I continue on the path to full recovery, I am pleased to say, "I have not been disappointed." There have been times of disappointment and ongoing challenges, but I have not been disappointed in the Lord's faithfulness to provide and meet the need that is confronting my life at the time.

Besides the issue of trust, I believe I have gained a greater appreciation of the grace and mercy of the Lord. Reading through the Old Testament, it can be easy to observe the failings of individuals and

God's people as a whole and be critical. However what we can learn is how the Lord truly is longsuffering, patient and full of mercy. That is something that should be an encouragement to our lives and something that should be extended to others.

The prophet Jeremiah declared in Lamentations, *"The steadfast love of the LORD never ceases; his mercies never come to an end; they are new every morning; great is your faithfulness. 'The LORD is my portion,' says my soul, 'therefore I will hope in him'"* (Lamentations 3:22-25 ESV). Each day brings new opportunities and new challenges. The Lord is a God of "all hope" (confident expectation). We can focus on the hope God gives. We can face each day with the assurance that God is with us.

Besides our trust and faith in the Lord being encouraged through scripture, my family has always connected with special songs for "special seasons." In the early days of my hospitalization, Debbie heard a song by Love and the Outcome, titled, "He is with Us." She quickly embraced that song as the "theme song" for my health crisis. The words of the song are a reminder that God is with us, always. Even when the road is dark and the future is uncertain we are called to know that God knows what He is doing and He will never leave or forsake us.

Life is filled with risks and dangers, joys and sorrows; don't go at it alone. We not only need assurance of the Lord's presence in our life, we also need others. We learned to trust God and we learned to trust others. Trusting others for me included medical professionals, family and friends. When crisis hits, many people "circle the wagons," but we choose to "open our arms." This certainly creates a great deal of anxiety, but it requires a different dimension of trust. Just as we trust God to work on our behalf, we needed to trust others to work for our good.

For us that included allowing family members to enter into our lives to handle finances, to take over projects that were "left hanging," to accept help from maintaining the house and yard to caring for grandchildren. We needed to allow others to enter the "personal space" of our life in order to have the support need that would permit Debbie to give her attention to my needs and advocate for my care. We needed to trust the insight of doctors and other caregivers at the various stages of recovery.

Through our experience we found over the years of life and ministry, we had sown into the lives of others. Those seeds of relationship and support for others produced a harvest of support and encouragement for our lives when it was needed the most.

## A Fresh Commitment to What Matters Most

When I reflect on my life, much of what I envisioned and hoped for has come my way. It was always an honor to be "called" to a church as a pastor knowing I was chosen over others who had expressed interest in serving a particular congregation. Having the opportunity to serve in the Colorado General Assembly as one of 100 out of five million in the State of Colorado is a humbling experience. When I realize how many have sought that goal and not achieved it, I don't take it for granted. The experiences of life with all the opportunities and challenges I view as a gift from the Lord.

However, when I faced days of uncertainty and life as I knew it came to a halt, it was my faith and relationship with the Lord, the commitment of my family and the support of friends that gave me a reason to live and the motivation to take one day at a time. As I began to develop my political website into a personal website for my devotional writings, I modified what had been my campaign logo to include the words, "Faith, Family and Friends." We now have the words stenciled on the wall of our family room that say, *"This Home is Built on Faith, Family and Friends."*

I have found much in life is fleeting. What we view as our security today can be gone tomorrow. What we have placed our trust in may prove to be "sinking sand." What did I discover when health, position and status was removed and life itself was in jeopardy? I found the true foundation in my life and came to understand more than ever its significance and that my commitment needed to be focused on my faith in God and in my relationship with my family and friends.

60<sup>th</sup> birthday

Therapy Rehab Hospital

regular clothes first time in four months

ready to go home – Sam Schmidt, Gwen and Phyllis Kovak,
Steve Harris, Bob Strauch

"Code: Ken" saying "goodbye" and "thank you."

Supporters gathered to celebrate homecoming 12/10/2013

Therapy chair provided by House Members

Family picture Christmas 2013

Leaving hospital again 12/16/2013 – Sue and Sam Schmidt, Tom and Judy Price

My mother and sister visit me at home

Softball teammates

With Rep. Spencer Swalm and House Sergeant Leon Brandli

Day by Day Sunday School class

return visit to the floor of the Colorado House

Additional pictures available at
http://www.caringbridge.org/visit/kensummers/photos and
http://kensummers.org/?page_id=24

# ENCOURAGEMENT AND INSPIRATION FROM THE ROAD TO RECOVERY

## Three Bedrock Truths about God

### BIBLE VERSE FOR TODAY...

*"The Lord is good. His mercy endures forever. His faithfulness endures throughout every generation."* (Psalm 100:5, GW)

This verse is not unique to this chapter, but is a refrain that is found often in the Psalms. The repetition of these phrases is something that should get our attention. Why not repeat these three lines of praise and allow them to sink into your heart. Consider each truth:

**The Lord is good.** This declaration points to the fundamental character of God. He is good. In the New Testament John declared, *"God is light in Him is no darkness at all"* (1 John 1:5, NKJV).

The goodness of God is not open for debate; it is (as we say in political parliamentary procedure) a settled question. The enemy of our souls wants us to view the circumstances of life, the condition of our world and bring into the question the character, the goodness of God. Don't allow those doubts to enter your mind. As you thank the Lord for His goodness, you will find strength and encouragement to face each day and any problem you will face.

**His mercy endures forever.** If mercy means, "I don't get what I do deserve," I need that every day! The Lord's compassion and His love for us allow us to live our lives not trusting in our own abilities or goodness. Instead we find daily strength that comes from God and the power of His Spirit working in our lives. Without His mercy we would be doomed: *"The steadfast love of the LORD never ceases; his mercies never come to an end; they are new every morning; great is your faithfulness"* (Lamentations 3:22-23, NIV).

**His faithfulness endures through every generation.** What God has been, He will be. What He has done, He will do. What He has promised, He will fulfill. He will be there for us, for our children, for our grandchildren, our great-grandchildren—every generation can know God's faithfulness to forgive, provide, direct, empower, restore, heal—the list can go on.

Our task is to reinforce in our own lives and in the lives of our loved ones all that the Lord is and provides. Remember three simple but power truths: The Lord is good! His mercy endures forever! His faithfulness endures through every generation!

## Charging God with Wrong

### BIBLE VERSE FOR TODAY...

> *"Then Job arose and tore his robe and shaved his head*
> *and fell on the ground and worshiped. And he said,*
> *'Naked I came from my mother's womb, and naked*
> *shall I return. In all this Job did not sin or charge*
> *God with wrong."* (Job 1:20-22, ESV)

Family, wealth and health. These three constitute that which makes our life worth living: the quality of life, the ability to enjoy life and the connection to our lineage. Job lost all three.

In the first phase of loss, Job lost his children, servants and his wealth. His wife would soon call on him to curse God and die. I used to be hard on Job's wife until I learned from my illness how stress and hardship can take a toll on family members, especially a spouse. The response of Job's wife was probably more normal than we realize. .

Job's response is instructive. His well-known response, *"The Lord gave, and the Lord has taken away; blessed be the name of the Lord"* can make it sound like Job, "took everything in stride." Yet, what we see is he showed the signs of intense grief, yet in his grief he turned to the Lord. Out of his focus on the Lord, he clung to that which is eternal, and he showed what he had, even his own children, he held loosely. He recognized all that he had came from God. He realized God gives, God takes, but in it all, God is to be honored.

What catches my attention is the statement, *"Job did not sin or charge God with wrong."* When hardship comes in whatever form and in whatever degree of intensity, it makes us vulnerable to become angry with God. Anger is often expressed in sinful behavior or blaming God as the source of our problems. We feel the Lord should keep us from any harm, loss or difficulty.

I recall reading an account of a pioneer missionary over 100 years ago who went to the Congo with a young wife. After his wife gave birth, she contracted malaria and died. The missionary gave his infant daughter to another missionary couple, returned to the U.S. and turned to a life of alcoholism, forbidding anyone to talk about God in his presence.

I recall visiting with a medical staff member during my initial hospital stay, who confessed to me that she was *"still mad at God"* over the death of her father. (I wanted to asked her, "How's that working out for you?!" but kept my traumatic brain injury thoughts from being spoken out loud.)

Obviously the examples are endless. I share these examples to demonstrate the challenge of a proper and healthy response to hardship and difficulties did not end with Job. Unfortunately, it appears the shipwrecks of faith outnumber those who strap themselves to the mast and ride out the storm to safety.

The bottom line to remember is, loss hurts, the pain is real and the grief must be confronted. It is okay to question and it is okay to be mad at God, He can handle it. In the end, after the storm waves begin to calm, you can find assurance in the words of Job: *"blessed by the name of the Lord"* (Job 1:21, NKJV). We see at the end of Job, the Lord restored all that he had lost and more.

When all is gone, hope is not gone if we realize the Lord is with us. I am reminded of the words of Peter, *"Lord, to whom shall we go? You have the words of eternal life"* (John 6:68, NIV). Jesus had no immediate family. He had no wealth. In the end, He suffered gruesome torture and death as one betrayed and falsely accused, but God gave Him new life and God can do that for you.

**Confidence in God**

**BIBLE VERSE FOR TODAY...**

> *"And this is the confidence that we have toward him,*
> *that if we ask anything according to his will he hears*
> *us. And if we know that he hears us in whatever we*
> *ask, we know that we have the requests that we have*
> *asked of him."* (1 John 5:14-15, ESV)

This is a verse that can inspire faith but at the same time solicit some inward conflict. Prayer is the way we cultivate our relationship with God. Prayer is the avenue by which we see the hand of God intervene in the affairs of God's people. One thing we know, 100 percent of the prayers that are not prayed go unanswered.

The key point is confidence before God is related to the fact that God hears us when we pray according to His will. John stretches the recesses of our faith by saying, *"If we know that He hears us . . . we know that we have . . . that we have asked of him."*

The great and sometimes nagging question becomes, *"What is God's will?"* I don't believe we can be 100 percent sure of God's will in every circumstance that confronts us, but we can pray in accordance to God's will. Let me try to explain my perspective.

**God's will is for everyone to come to faith in Him.** *"[Christ] wants everyone to be saved and to understand the truth."* (1 Timothy 2:4, NLT)

**God's will for everyone is to have confidence of their eternal destiny.** *"I write these things to you who believe in the name of the Son of God that you may know that you have eternal life."* (1 John 5:13, NIV)

**God's will is for us to be totally committed to Him**. *"God's will is for you to be holy."* (1 Thessalonians 4:3, NLT)

**God's will is for us to know the work of the Holy Spirit in our life.** *"...though you are evil, know how to give good gifts to your children, how much more will your Father in heaven give the Holy Spirit to those who ask him!"* (Luke 11:13, NIV)

**God's will is for us to pray for the sick.** *"They [Jesus' followers] will be able to place their hands on the sick, and they will be healed."*(Mark 16:18, NLT) *"...prayer of faith shall save him that is sick, and the Lord shall raise him up."* (James 5:15)

**God's will is for us to know His will.** *"By this we shall know that we are of the truth and reassure our heart before him; for whenever our heart condemns us, God is greater than our heart, and he knows everything. Beloved, if our heart does not condemn us, we have confidence before God; and whatever we ask we receive from him..."* (1 John 3:19-22, ESV)

At times our human desires can get in the way of understanding and praying God's will. Even Jesus in the garden prayed, *"not my will, but yours be done"* (Luke 22:42, NIV). Sometimes, as John puts it, *"our hearts can condemn us,"* because we find our prayers are filled with *our* needs and *our* desires. We spend too much time treating the Lord as a cosmic Santa Claus instead of coming to Him to "learn of Him" to cultivate our relationship with Him and simply "abide in Him." Jesus said, *"If you abide in me, and my words abide in you, ask whatever you wish, and it will be done for you"* (John 15:7, NIV).

The foundational concept is, "when we pray in agreement with God's *Word*, we pray in agreement with God's *will*." As we learn God's Word, as we "pray God's Word," as we learn of those who sought the Lord in the Bible, it encourages our faith and empowers our confidence. . I have found as I seek the Lord, He will always give me what I need, even if He doesn't give me what I want.

## Down But Not Out

**BIBLE VERSE FOR TODAY...**

*"Do not gloat over me, my enemy! Though I have fallen, I will rise. Though I sit in darkness, the Lord will be my light."* (Micah 7:8, NIV)

The prophet Micah personifies Israel and God's judgment on His people as he opens Chapter 7 with this lament: *"What misery is mine...The faithful have been swept from the land; not one upright person remains. Everyone lies in wait to shed blood; they hunt each other with nets. Both hands are skilled in doing evil..."* (Micah 7:1-3, NIV).

We observe while God's judgment is upon His people, the promise of restoration is also clearly seen. There are those who have watched from the sidelines and looked at Israel like it is their final hour, but the assurance is sounded, *"I will rise again."* Not only that, but those who have ridiculed God's people themselves be judged when God's people are restored.

*"Then my enemy will see it and will be covered with shame, she who said to me, 'Where is the Lord your God?' My eyes will see her downfall; even now she will be trampled underfoot like mire in the streets"* (Micah 7:10, NIV).

Even in the midst of judgment, while the heavy hand of the Lord upon His people, they knew their true source of strength. Their confidence of rising back up and the light breaking through the darkness comes from hope in the Lord.

*"But as for me, I watch in hope for the Lord, I wait for God my Savior; my God will hear me"* (Micah 7:7, NIV).

Micah 7 ends on an encouraging note of prayer and praise to the Lord: *"Who is a God like you ... You do not stay angry forever but delight to show mercy. You will again have compassion on us; you will tread our sins underfoot and hurl all our iniquities into the depths of the sea"* (Micah 7:18-19, NIV).

How do we have confidence that when we are down, we are not out? We can learn from the words of Micah. Our hope must always be in the Lord and we must realize He hears our cry for forgiveness and mercy. Then we realize the Lord is a God of compassion and mercy. As we submit to Him and place our trust in Him, we realize this assurance, *"For I will forgive their wickedness and will remember their sins no more"* (Hebrews 8:12, NIV).

When we fall, the Lord allows us to rise again; but it is to a new path, a new hope and a new life; one that is lived in the light of His presence.

**Eternal God – Everlasting Encouragement**

### BIBLE VERSE FOR TODAY...

*"The eternal God is your refuge, and underneath are the everlasting arms."* (Deuteronomy 33:27, NKJV)

This statement of encouragement from Moses as the Children of Israel prepared to enter the Promised Land holds encouragement for followers of Christ today. In this one statement, there are some noteworthy points to grab and hold on to.

**1 – An Endless Resource** – *"The eternal God."* The one who provides strength for your journey and is available to meet your need is the God who was and is and will always be! Jesus said, *"Heaven and earth will pass away, but my words will never pass away"* (Matthew 24:35, NIV). God's promise is, *"never will I leave you, never will I forsake you"* (Hebrews 13:5, NIV). You can't escape Him, you won't exhaust His patience and you will never be outside of His love.

**2 – An Encompassing Protection** – *"God is your refuge."* One of the repeated images of God in the Old Testament is that of a refuge. The psalmist declared, *"God is my refuge and strength an ever-present help in time of trouble"* (Psalm 46:1, NIV). *"God is my refuge and fortress"* (Psalm 91:2, NIV). *"As the mountains surround Jerusalem, so the Lord surrounds His people both now and forevermore"* (Psalm 125:2, NIV). The hymn writer of old referred to the Lord as, "A shelter in the time of storm." A refuge speaks of protection, comfort and assurance. A refuge is only as good as it is used. As Jesus prepared to leave His disciples He admonished them, *"Trust in God, trust also in me"* (John 14:1, NIV).

**3 – An Enduring Encouragement** – *"Underneath are the everlasting arms."* This is a great picture of security and safety. Talk about the "wind beneath my wings." I recently saw a couple of cartoon captions that caught my attention. In one, Jesus says to the person next to Him, "When you see one set of footprints in the sand that is when I carried you." The next frame Jesus says, "When you see the groove, that is when I drug you kicking and screaming." I am not sure about the theology behind that, but it does show the Lord doesn't give up on us and is with us even when we are not eager followers.

> *"If I ascend to heaven, you are there! If I make my bed in Sheol, you are there! If I take the wings of the morning and dwell in the uttermost parts of the sea, even there your hand shall lead me, and your right hand shall hold me"* (Psalm 139:8-10, ESV).

When it comes to needing a refuge and source of strength, don't settle for anything less than the best.

## Expecting the Unexpected

### BIBLE VERSE FOR TODAY...

*"Who shall separate us from the love of Christ? Shall tribulation, or distress, or persecution, or famine, or nakedness, or danger, or sword?...in all these things we are more than conquerors through him who loved us ... [nothing] will be able to separate us from the love of God in Christ Jesus our Lord."* (Romans 8:35,37,39, NIV)

As we look at familiar verses and promises in God's Word, we are reminded the reality of those promises is experienced the most when the unexpected comes; when the crisis happens. When tribulations, distress, persecution, famine, nakedness, danger come they can make us "feel" separated from God's love. These times and circumstances test the mettle of our faith, trust and focus.

As I near my first anniversary date for my return home from the hospital, I am reflecting on some aspects of life and the "unexpected."

1 – **The unexpected is part of life.** We understand that. We don't expect it to happen to us! No one expects to get a cancer diagnosis, have a health crisis, be in an accident, have a family crisis or have something happen to their children. We plan for the unexpected to a degree when we buy life insurance, when businesses establish succession plans – we just don't believe they will ever be needed. For a vast number of people, that may be true, but it doesn't mean people don't experience the unexpected lay-off or other financial crisis. An acquaintance of mine is still working in his late seventies because of a financial loss occurred through a much publicized company

147

scandal. Through no fault of his own, his plans for a less active retirement were changed.

**2 – The unexpected is a challenge.** During a crisis, decisions must be made, priorities reassessed, schedules changed and additional expenses are incurred when income is diminished. These are some of the logistics of dealing with crisis. Then there is the challenge of "dealing with the crisis." The toll on emotions, family members and others in our circle of relationships can be significant.

When I reflect on my illness and hospitalization, it is difficult for me to comprehend the toll and challenge faced by my family. There was not only the concern for what happened to me, but the challenge of rearranging schedules and jumping in to handle even day-to-day matters of the house and paying bills. From my perspective, it appeared there was as much happening around me as there was happening to me.

When facing the challenge of the unexpected, help is needed. Crisis is a time to open your life, not "circle the wagons" and shut yourself off and "go at it alone." That was one area where Debbie acted decisively and with wisdom. Psychiatrist Victor Frankl said, "When we are no longer able to change a situation, we are challenged to change ourselves."

**3 – The unexpected is a test.** For the record, I hate tests! However, when a crisis comes, it presents a test, a test that must be faced and a test that must be passed. This of course is more of a "pop quiz" because you don't know when it is coming.

The unexpected is a test of our trust in the Lord. It is a test of our trust in God's love, God's provision, God's direction and God's ability to help us to deal with the challenge before us. Author Mary Engelbreit said, "If you don't like it, change it; if you can't change it;

change the way you think about it." The Lord can help us with that and sometimes that is the greatest miracle.

Proverbs 3:5-6 applies to these situations more than we recognize: *"Trust in the Lord with all your heart, and do not lean on your own understanding. In all your ways acknowledge him, and he will make straight your paths."*

The unexpected can test our ways and our will. Crisis calls for change and change is difficult. Sometimes it is helpful to evaluate our thoughts and feelings by replacing "can't" with "won't."

I **can't** let others help me. I **won't** let others help me.

I **can't** let go of_____. I **won't** let go of _____.

I **can't** deal with this! I **won't** deal with this!

I **can't** forgive. I **won't** forgive.

I believe you get the point. When we say we believe with Paul, *"I can do all things through Christ who gives me strength"*(Philippians 4:13), we will find the unexpected tests how extensive our belief is in "all things." Often the miracle the Lord brings to our crisis is how He changes us in our situation and provides us the strength and peace beyond our ability.

## From Bitterness to Blessing

### BIBLE VERSE FOR TODAY...

*"I went away full, but the Lord has brought me back empty. Why do you call me Naomi when the Lord has tormented me and the Almighty has done evil to me?"* (Ruth 1:21, GW) *"The Lord hasn't stopped being kind to people—living or dead."* (Ruth 2:20, GW)

This brief book is somewhat of an interlude in the historic account of Israel moving into the Promised Land. It is significant because at the end of the story we find Ruth, an emigrant to Israel from Moab, becomes the great-grandmother of King David.

The story could be named after Naomi, because much of the story focuses around her and her influence on the life of Ruth. This is especially true after Ruth leaves her own country to follow Naomi back to Bethlehem.

Briefly, Naomi and her husband and two sons go to Moab during a time of famine in Israel. In Moab, her husband dies. Her sons marry and ten years later, they die. Naomi is alone without husband or sons. She decides to return to Israel hearing the famine has come to an end. Her daughter-in-laws decide to leave their country and stay with Naomi. Naomi implores them to go back to their own country. Orpah, after an emotional time of decision, returns home, but Ruth is determined to stake her future with Naomi and a new home in Israel.

Ruth is sent out by Naomi to glean wheat and barley in the fields of a wealthy landowner by the name of Boaz. The ensuing events find Boaz, a relative to Naomi's husband, marrying Ruth to preserve the family name in Israel. Ruth has a son named Obed who has a son named Jesse who has a son named David.

That is the quick summary of a biblical love story. What caught my attention during this reading was Naomi's perspective of her life and what she went through. When Naomi returned to Bethlehem, she did so without her husband, sons and only her daughter-in-law. She had endured great loss after thinking she and her husband years ago had made a good decision for their family.

When she returned to her friends and hometown, people were excited to see her, but this is what she said, *"Don't call me Naomi [Sweet]. Call me Mara [Bitter] because the* **Almighty has made my life very bitter.** *I went away full, but the Lord has brought me back empty. Why do you call me Naomi when the* **Lord has tormented me and the Almighty has done evil to me?"** (Ruth 1:20-21, GW).

Later, when Naomi found out Ruth had been gathering grain in the field of Boaz, her perspective changed. She said, *"May the Lord bless him.* **The** *Lord hasn't stopped being kind to people—living or dead* ... *That man is a relative of ours. He is a close relative, one of those responsible for taking care of us"* (Ruth 2:20, GW).

What a change in attitude and perspective! As the story unfolds, you can see Naomi's faith and confidence in God's care and provision begins to rekindle. At the end of the story with the birth of Obed, the Bible says, *"Naomi took the child, held him in her lap and became his guardian"* (Ruth 4:16, GW).

What a turnaround for Naomi, from blaming God to blessing God, to having no family to being the guardian of the ancestor of King David.

Based on this story, I would challenge you to keep the following in mind:

1 – Don't make hasty conclusions about your life, or God.

2 – Regardless of how you may view the events of your life, God will not abandon you or stop working for your good.

3 – Don't write the conclusion of your story while God is still writing your story.

> *"We consider those who endure to be blessed. You have heard about Job's endurance. You saw that the Lord ended Job's suffering because the Lord is compassionate and merciful"* (James 5:11, GW).

I'm not sure how often I have heard the advice, "Let's wait and see what happens." It is usually a reminder to not "jump to a conclusion" or "don't act too hastily" or "let's see what others do." That is good advice as we live our life confident in God's provision and care. It will keep us from becoming bitter while we wait for the blessing.

**When What I Fear Happens**

**BIBLE VERSE FOR TODAY....**
> *"For the thing that I fear comes upon me, and what I
> dread befalls me."* (Job 3:25, ESV)

This statement is from Job's first "discourse" after not only losing children, servants and livestock, but also his health. It is Job's physical suffering that makes his wife say, *"Curse God and die"* (Job 2:9, ESV).

This verse contains an idiom that we still hear today: *"What I feared has come upon me."* I am not sure if modern psychology would attribute this to "self-fulfilling prophecy" or a bazaar occurrence. It is true that ninety-nine percent of the things we worry about don't happen. That is why worry is unproductive; still there are those scenarios that all of us have in our mind that we would not want to face.

For me, an extended hospital stay with tubes running out of all my body cavities was one of those. As a pastor I had seen people in all types of serious conditions in ICU units and hospital rooms. That exposure was probably the reason for my "I-don't-ever-want-to-be-in-that-situation" list.

I received the email one morning about the man with West Nile Virus whose situation was similar to mine. With the exception of his diabetes (not sure how serious), he played golf, was an active member of his church and in good physical condition. I am sure for a man in his mid-seventies, he would have expected some other health crisis other than one from being bit by a mosquito. I am familiar with men like this outplaying me on my senior softball team.

Here are some things I have learned about facing the unexpected:

153

**When we face the unexpected, our faith is put to the test.** Faith is only revealed in the midst of the test or the fight. Peter talks about the "trying of our faith" (1 Peter 1:7). Paul writes about the "shield of faith" that distinguishes the enemy's (Satan's) arrows (Ephesians 6:16).

**When we face the unexpected, we find strength to meet the need.** I have found you don't realize what you can go through until you have to go through it. Paul, in pleading with Jesus about his "thorn in the flesh," received the message of reassurance from the Lord: *"My power is made perfect in weakness."* Paul goes on and makes a statement of contrast, *"when I am weak, then am I strong"* (2 Corinthians 12:9-10, NLT). I like the adage that says, "God doesn't give dying grace on non-dying days."

**When we face the unexpected, it reveals our character.** Job's wife asked him, "Will you still hold on to your integrity?" The reality is, when all is stripped away, that is all that you have. A recent issue of *Reader's Digest* contained an article by retired Navy SEAL Mark Divine titled, "Learning to Take a Stand." Divine, speaking from a career in the military and business, says, "I've noticed that leadership is not skill. It's character. Successful, happy, and fulfilled people embody core values such as honor, courage and commitment to personal excellence." This applies to whether you are leading a troop, company, family or yourself. Just as hot water brings out the flavor and color of the tea, so do the "hot water" circumstances of life bring out what is inside of us.

I am thankful the Lord is faithful to give strength in the midst of the tests of life that build and reveal our character. Just as the Lord's love and faithfulness endures forever, so our faith must endure in good times and in bad, in sickness and in health.

*Note: This was written on the first anniversary of my hospitalization.*
**Blame God or Fear God?**

**BIBLE VERSE FOR TODAY...**
> *"When a man's folly brings his way to ruin, his heart rages against the Lord ... The fear of the Lord leads to life, and whoever has it rests satisfied; he will not be visited by harm."* (Proverbs 19:3,23)

From time to time, I am reminded how insightful scripture is to the character of people. I am also reminded how little people have changed over the course of time. In my life, interacting with people I don't know how many times someone expresses anger, resentment or disillusionment with God over something they were responsible for. They have the attitude, "if I am not supposed to do this, God will stop me." These are not individuals who necessarily even claim to be people of faith.

My conclusion this morning when I read Proverbs 19:3 was, "People have always been the same." Their own actions get them in trouble, but it is God's fault. "God let me down; where was God?!"

Later in Proverbs 19, we read how an individual can have confidence before God. The key is the "fear of the Lord." That means allowing our life to be directed by the Lord, staying close to Him, loving what He loves, hating what He hates. That is where we find life, rest and safety.

Don't "pass the buck;" don't blame God when your own actions lead to harm. Instead, look to Him for wisdom and commit your life to Him. Then you will find He is there to guide, protect and rescue you from all harm. Remember to journey with the Lord through all of life, not just in times of need or desperation. Our aim should be that which is reflected in the words of Peter, *"But grow in the grace and knowledge of our Lord and Savior Jesus Christ. To him be the glory both now and to the day of eternity. Amen"* (2 Peter 3:18).

## Mountain Size Trust

### BIBLE VERSE FOR TODAY...

> "Those *who trust in the Lord are like Mount Zion,*
> *which cannot be moved, but abides forever. As the*
> *mountains surround Jerusalem, so the Lord sur-*
> *rounds his people, from this time forth and forever-*
> *more."* (Psalm 125:1-2, NIV)

We often hear of "mountain moving" faith. Yet we find in Psalm 125, one of the "Psalms of Ascent," a reference to our trust in the Lord being like Mount Zion. The imagery is clear and significant. Trusting in the Lord brings stability to life. In an ocean of uncertainty, the one thing we can do to bring steadfastness to our world is to trust in the Lord. Trust and do not be afraid. Trust and do not waver.

Trust is needed when we don't understand and when we face challenges beyond ourselves. (Sounds like every day.) Trust is the companion of faith. When God called Abraham, he believed God, and he trusted in God to do what God had promised. You will discover, like I have, that is what the Christian life is all about. We are called to go without knowing all the details and having the journey neatly mapped out before us.

Trust provides a confidence to our life. Notice the psalmist says, "Those who trust in the **Lord**" are like Mount Zion. We can and do place our trust in various places—our friends, our financial security, our government (sometimes), our spouse. Yet, it is only trust in the Lord that brings true stability and confidence. At one time I would say I trusted in my health. I used to go see my family physician every two or three years because of some strep or flu-type symptoms and because we were both from the same high school. While I had some issues that appear to crop up with age and stress my body incurred in my running years, I did not have or expect any challenging issues with my health. I found trusting in the reliability of your health can lead to disappointment.

The second verse of Psalm 125 provides the reason for the assurance of our trust. *"As the mountains surround Jerusalem so the Lord surrounds His people."* This reminds me of the time the Assyrians came against the prophet Elisha and his servant trembled in fear. Elisha prayed for the servant's eyes to be opened. *"Then the Lord opened the eyes of the young man, and he saw. And behold, the mountain was full of horses and chariots of fire all around Elisha"* (2 Kings 6:17, ESV).

Trust in the Lord enables us to see the natural through supernatural eyes.

- When doubts and fears arise, just trust.
- When finances are in a crisis, just trust.
- When the doctor's report is negative, just trust.
- When your kids are struggling, just trust.
- When relationships are on the rocks, just trust.
- When the job you counted on comes to an end, just trust.
- When God calls you to a God-sized cause, just trust.

As you do, you will find the Lord surrounding you now and forevermore!

## Living Through Preparing to Die

### BIBLE VERSE FOR TODAY...

*"One dies in his full vigor, being wholly at ease and secure, his pails full of milk and the marrow of his bones moist. Another dies in bitterness of soul, never having tasted of prosperity. They lie down alike in the dust, and the worms cover them."* (Job 21:23-26, ESV)

Death is not something that is easy to talk about, especially your own. With my work as a pastor and Debbie's work as a hospice nurse, death has been a part of our world. When our daughter Stephanie graduated from college, her first job was working for a funeral home in Cleveland, Tennessee. Many were surprised to find someone so young working with families at the time of grief and helping families prearrange their funerals. She would explain, "My dad is a pastor and my mother a hospice nurse so it felt natural."

Not everyone is as comfortable with the topic. Some take the approach, "I'll deal with it when it happens." Others take a more reflective approach. What we see expressed in the words of Job is death is the great equalizer. Whether you live in a mansion or a humble home, death brings the same end for everyone. For some, death is tragic and quick; for some, it is prolonged and painful.

Death requires preparation. That *"preparation"* may be processing your own mortality, as well as practical and spiritual ramifications of death. We read in the Bible the well-known words, *"set your house in order"* as a prelude to death. The idea of thinking about your own mortality leads to the practical and spiritual preparations.

On the practical side, there are tools that can help guide family members in the desires of a loved one who is facing death or an extended illness. Some of those include a medical power of attorney, a general power of attorney and a document called "Five Wishes." (See End Notes.) Debbie and I remember doing that with her mother a few weeks before she became critically ill. The decisions made during that time, helped Debbie and her sister know their actions were in keeping with what their mom had expressed.

The Bible is clear that, *"it is appointed for man to die once, and after that comes judgment"* (Hebrews 9:27, ESV). Preparing for your death financially and practically is a blessing to your family. When the time comes, your family will have those who will support and provide as much assistance as possible. However, only **you** can make the spiritual preparations that are needed for death. That is why the best known verse of the Bible contains the words, *"that whoever believes in him [Jesus] should not perish but have eternal life"* (John 3:16, NIV).

The Lord makes provision for your life from birth to beyond death. His desire is for those who place their faith in Him, to be with Him forever. That is why the Apostle Paul asserts with confidence, *"to be absent from the body is to be present with the Lord"* (2 Corinthians 5:8, NIV). That is why Paul said, *[Nothing] "...in all creation, will be able to separate us from the love of God in Christ Jesus our Lord"* (Romans 8:39, ESV).

How are your preparations for that inevitable day? What you will find is that those who are the most prepared to die, are those who are the most prepared to live!

**God's View of You**

**BIBLE VERSE FOR TODAY...**

> *"The Lord your God is with you. He is a hero who saves*
> *you. He happily rejoices over you, renews you with*
> *his love, and celebrates over you with shouts of joy."*
> (Zephaniah 3:17, GW)

The prophet Zephaniah traces his family lineage back to Judah's righteous King Hezekiah. He spoke his word of prophecy during the reign of King Josiah, who listened to the prophets more than any other king and lead the people in a time returning to the Lord.

The three short chapters of this book contain God's judgment on the earth, judgment on Judah and a call to *"search for the Lord ... and find shelter in the day of the Lord's anger."* We also see the promised restoration of God's people after this time of discipline. As stern as the words of judgment, the words of the prophet provide hope and a future for God's people.

> *"Celebrate and rejoice with all your heart, people of*
> *Jerusalem. The Lord has reversed the judgments against*
> *you. He has forced out your enemies. The king of Israel,*
> *the Lord, is with you."* (Zephaniah 3:15 GW)

The crescendo of these words of reassurance (v.17) reinforces the fact that *"God is with you. ... He ... saves you. He ... rejoices over you ... renews you ... and celebrates over you with shouts of joy."*

Whether walking in victory or facing times of struggle and challenge, your view of God is vitally important. What is important to remember is your view of God is impacted when you understand **His** view of you. If there is one thing that comes across in this verse, it is exactly that!

# End Notes and Resources

Chapter 4 – "Mosquito Borne Disease," American Mosquito Control Association, Accessed September 15, 2015, http://www.mosquito.org/mosquito-borne-diseases

"West Nile Virus," Colorado Mosquito Control, Accessed September 15, 2015, http://www.comosquitocontrol.com/West_Nile_Virus.html

"West Nile Virus Statistics." Larimer County, Accessed September 15, 2015, https://larimer.org/health/cd/stats.htm

Note: Larimer County, Colorado reported 89 confirmed cases of human West Nile Virus infections in 2013.

Chapter 6 – Tim Brotzman, *From Victim to Victor – Whiner to Winner – Pitiful to Powerful*. (Grand Rapids: WestBow Press, 2016)

(Note: Tim is a radio personality and businessman who has faced the devastation of body and relationships. He provides practical insights and guidelines to those facing any kind of tragedy in life.)

Chapter 10 – Mark Batterson, *The Circle Maker*. (Grand Rapids: Zondervan Publishing, 2011) pg. 13

Chris Rademake, Jodi King, Seth Mosely. *"His is With Us"* © 2002, Word Music, ARR, UBP

## Devotionals:

Mark Batterson, *All In* (Grand Rapid: Zondervan Publishing 2013) pg. 123-124

End of Life Resources – Five Wishes–https://fivewishesonline.aging-withdignity.org/

The Conversation Project–www.theconversationproject.org

"It's Your Choice", Mary Engelbreit, Accessed March 15, 2015, www.brhttps://hyla1880.wordpress.com/tag/mary-engelbreit/

Brainy Quotes, Victor Frankel, Accessed March 15, 2015, http://www.brainyquote.com/quotes/quotes/v/viktorefr121087.html

Mark Divine, *"Learning to Take a Stand,"* Readers Digest, August 2014, pg 95

# Additional Resources:

You Tube video "My Story" https://www.youtube.com/watch?v=JQmnkEhxzDg

Media Reports can be found through an internet search: "Ken Summers West Nile Virus"

Caring Bridge – www.CaringBridge.org is a website for individuals facing a health crisis to share updates and progress reports with family members and friends. It served as a vital tool as many across the country were interested in my status and how they could pray and support.

**Ken's West Nile Timeline**
June 30, 2013 – Move into home in Fort Collins
July 22, 2013 – Admitted to McKee Hospital, Loveland
July 25, 2013 – Diagnosed with encephalitis caused by West Nile Virus
July 29, 2013 – Meningitis diagnosis confirmed
July 30, 3013 – Respiratory failure and move to ICU (life support)
August 3, 2013 – Feeding tube inserted
August 6, 2013 – Tracheotomy

August 10, 2013–Myasthenia Gravis diagnosis confirmed

August 11, 2013 – Plasmapharesis treatments begin (five treatments every other day)

August 16, 2013 – Taken outside in wheelchair for first time

August 19, 2013 – Transfer to Northern Colorado Long Term Acute Hospital

August 27, 2013 – PICC line inserted

August 28, 2013 – First shower in special chair

September 1, 2013 – Aspiration episode with feeding tube procedure (September 5 was planned surgery day)

September 6, 2013 – Sitting up in wheelchair

September 11, 2013 – Stood in "standing frame" for first time

September 17, 2013 – Off "life support" – exercise in wheelchair

September 23, 2013 – Move back to McKee Hospital

September 26, 2013 – Surgery

October 5, 2013 – Haircut at hospital able to sit on bed without support

October 7, 2013 – Move back to Long Term Acute Hospital

October 10, 2013 – Move to Northern Colorado Rehabilitation Hospital

October 12, 2013 – Able to reach the top of my head for first time

November 12, 2013 – Celebrate 60th birthday in hospital

December 10, 2013 – Leave Rehabilitation Hospital for home!

December 13, 2013 – Admitted to McKee Hospital with infection

December 16, 2013 – Leave McKee Hospital for home

December 17, 2013 – Begin homebound therapy and IV antibiotics for infection

December 24, 2013 – Attend Christmas Eve service with family

January 7, 2014 – First steps with walker

February 7, 2014 – Visited Colorado House and attended Drug Task Force Meeting in Denver

February 22, 2014 – Septic shock, admitted to Poudre Valley Hospital (ICU)

February 25, 2014 – Transfer to regular room at Poudre Valley Hospital

February 27, 2014 – Transfer to Northern Colorado Rehabilitation Hospital

March 9, 2014 – Leave Rehabilitation Hospital for home/continue IV antibiotics

April 2, 2014 – Test drive a car

April 17, 2014 – Begin to transition to a walker – navigate fifty feet

April 22-24, 2014 – Attend Church Conference in Grand Junction

May 2, 2014 – Invocation at Colorado House and begin outpatient therapy

May 9-10, 2014–Trip to Gunnison for niece's college graduation

May 16, 2014 – Perform wedding ceremony with son Christian

May 17, 2014 – Ride my wheelchair in the Colfax Charity 5k

May 20, 2014 – Hospitalized with infection

May 23, 2014 – Leave Hospital for home

June 29, 2014 – Speak at Southwest First Assembly

July 11, 2014 – Speak at So. Jeffco Rotary Club

July 12, 2014 – Outpatient treatment for major infection

July 18-20, 2014 – Attend Western Conservative Summit–Denver

July 30, 3014 – Return to Northern Colorado Rehabilitation Hospital to share in presentation of Tribute from Colorado House

August 3, 2014 – Visit Day by Day class at Southern Gables Church

August 20, 2014 – Admitted to McKee Hospital with infection

August 23, 2014 – Return home from hospital/continue IV antibiotics

October 12, 2014 – Share testimony at Red Rocks Fellowship, Littleton

October 31, 2014 – Begin fitness center workouts

December 14, 2014 – Video testimony shared at Timberline Church

January 7-13, 2014 – Trip to Atlanta by myself

July 17, 2014 – Share my experience with the Larimer County Board of Health

February 19, 2015 – Invocation at Colorado House

March 2, 2015 – Begin gradual transition to "Canadian" crutches

March 14, 2015 – Invocation at State Republican Central Committee Meeting

April 28, 2015 – Graduate from outpatient therapy

June 3, 2015 – Handicap ramp removed

July 18-23, 2015 – Attend "Grand Camp" with oldest grandson Riley

August 14, 2015 – Keynote speaker at Northern Colorado Rehabilitation Hospital 10th Anniversary

# About Author

Ken Summers is a Colorado native. He served twenty-eight years as a pastor, six years as a Colorado State Representative and seven years the Executive Director of Teen Challenge of the Rocky Mountains.

During his legislative service, he was recognized as the "Legislator of the Year" by the Colorado Nonprofit Association and the Colorado Medical Society honored him with their highest award, "The Protector the Patient." Ken served two years as the Chair of the House Health and Environment Committee.

In July 2013, following a move to Fort Collins, Colorado (after losing a bid for a seat in the Colorado State Senate), Ken was hospitalized with West Nile Virus. This lead to almost five months of hospitalization, followed by several hospital stays in 2014 to fight off major infections.

As Ken continues his recovery, he is serving as Co-Chair of the Larimer Energy Action Project and is still involved in public policy issues. In addition, he writes a devotional blog and conducts chapel services and Bible studies at local assisted living facilities and is a volunteer at Timberline Church.

Ken earned a BA in Business Education from the University of Northern Colorado and a Master of Nonprofit Management degree from Regis University. Ken is married to Debbie (a hospice nurse). They have two grown children, Christian (wife, Bridget) and Stephanie (husband, Nathan) and six grandchildren.